Cuban
Exile
Memories

JOURNEYS OF COURAGE AND RESILIENCE
IN THE PURSUIT OF FREEDOM

TALEK NANTES

First Edition

© 2021 Talek Nantes

Book cover and interior formatting by SusanasBooks LLC

Published by Excelsior Press

United States of America.
Follow Talek Nantes at:
www.travelswithtalek.com
www.facebook.com/travelswithtalek
Travelswithtalek@travelstalek
www.pinterest.com/travelstalek
www.instagram.com/travelswithtalek
All rights reserved.
Print ISBN: 978-0-578-83451-1
eBook ISBN: 978-0-578-82261-7

DEDICATION

For my mother and my husband, my two favorite Cubans, whose stories appear in these pages.

CONTENTS

DEFINITIONS

Brigada 2506 A group of Cuban exiles formed in 1960 to attempt the military overthrow of the Castro regime.

Camarioca Exodus A period in late 1965 when Cubans left the islands on boats destined for the United States.

Chivato A snitch, traitor.

CDR *Comité para la Defensa de La Revolución.* In English, Committee for the Defense for the Revolution, a neighborhood watch group encouraged to spy and report on neighbors perceived to be against the Revolution.

Efficiency apartment Small studio with limited kitchen.

Food ration book Government-issued ration book to purchase subsidized food in Cuba.

G2 Cuban secret police.

Gusano Literally "worm," but used to describe people who left Cuba fleeing communism.

La Cabaña Notorious Havana prison.

Los Reyes Magos: The Three Kings. January 6 holiday when Cuban children receive gifts.

Milicianos (nas) Revolutionary military personnel.

Paredón The firing squad.

Peter Pan organization An organization supported by the Catholic Church that brought Cuban children out of Cuba to the United States where they were reunited with their parents as soon as the parents could leave Cuba.

Rancho Boyeros The name of the Havana Airport during that period.

UMAP "Military Unit to Aid Production." Civilian labor service camp in Cuba for conscientious objectors, members of various religions, homosexuals, political enemies of Fidel Castro, and others.

Visa Waiver Document allowing Cubans to enter the United States.

INTRODUCTION

This book was written by Cuban exiles for Cuban exiles and for anyone interested in stories of courage and the pursuit of freedom. It is a collection of memories about the Cuban exile experience of the mid-20th century: a testament to the courage, persistence, and determination of people whose lives were upended quickly, dramatically, and irrevocably by a political movement.

These anonymized experiences tell of the sometimes-improbable circumstances that led a generation to leave their homeland and everything they knew to come to a foreign country and start their lives again from scratch.

The memories have been collected from anecdotes passed down over generations, interviews, and personal recollections. Many of the stories are in the speaker's own words, which sometimes revert to Spanish, and these are accompanied by English-language translations. Each story is told by a different exile sharing his or her own memory.

The main thread that runs through the book is the chaos and confusion of the communist takeover in Cuba and the subsequent exodus of a significant portion of the island's population. Also covered are the struggles and sacrifices the exiles made during the early years of arrival in their new countries as well as humorous examples of cultural clashes while attempting to adapt.

Lastly, this is a declaration of unabashed appreciation to the United States, the country that gave so many of us the opportunity to pursue our own destinies in peace and freedom.

PREFACE

The story of Miguel "Mike" Bezos leaving Cuba to escape Castro's communism and come to the United States is familiar to many Cubans.
Bezos came to the U.S. as a young man of sixteen in 1962. Like many Cubans, he came alone and spoke no English.

The Bezos family business had been seized and nationalized by the Castro regime, and the family lost everything they had worked for all their lives. During this time of upheaval, people who were not clearly in support of the Cuban Revolution were also being arrested— and worse. In fear for their son's safety, the Bezos family decided to send Mike to the States.

Like so many single Cuban children, Mike Bezos left Cuba through Operation Peter Pan, an organization supported by the Catholic Church and designed to send Cuban minors from six to eighteen to the United States. Their parents sent them because

rumors were flying that the new Communist government would terminate parental rights and indoctrinate all children in Communism. Once their children were outside Cuba and safe, the parents began planning to join them in the United States as soon as they were able to leave Cuba.

Believing that it was cold where Mike was going, his mother gathered rags and bits and pieces of fabric, and with her daughter's help, fashioned a coat for Mike to keep him warm in his new land. This coat was one of the few things he could bring on his exodus; it eventually became a family heirloom.

In a video celebrating the opening of the Statue of Liberty Museum on Liberty Island, Bezos recounts his story. "My parents were not allowed to go into the airport with me, so they dropped me off," said Mike. "I got on an airplane and landed in Miami forty-five minutes later. We could only bring with us three pairs of pants, three shirts, three pairs of underwear, and one pair of shoes."

Like most children, Mike Bezos first traveled to various locations in the U.S. before finally settling. He initially stayed in a refugee camp in Florida for over three weeks. From there, he traveled to Wilmington,

Delaware to attend high school. A determined young man with grades that improved along with his language skills, Mike soon had a scholarship to a college in Albuquerque, New Mexico.

"I had very little idea at that time where Albuquerque was," Mike remembers.

It was in Albuquerque where he met his future wife, Jackie, and her son Jeff. They soon married. Mike adopted Jeff and raised him as his own.

Today Mike's son, Jeff, is the richest man in the world—Jeff Bezos.

"It is truly unbelievable. I look back on my life, and I had *lived* the American Dream thirty years ago," Mike Bezos says. "It's really just out of this world."

Mike never returned to Cuba but maintained his Cuban identity and is said to still love Cuban food.

Although traumatic for a child, the experiences of Mike Bezos were not as harrowing as those of many other Cuban exiles. These are their stories.

PART 1 - WHEN I LEFT CUBA

PART 1
WHEN I LEFT CUBA

1

My father was a young man in 1949 when the Communist government rose to power and nationalized our wealthy family's businesses in Guangzhou in southern China. He did not believe there was opportunity for future growth under the new regime, so he emigrated to Cuba to join an uncle who had prospered there.

Havana's Chinatown was thriving. My dad established himself there and developed a restaurant business. In 1959, the Cuban Revolution succeeded in coming to power. My dad initially thought this would not be a repeat of the Chinese Revolution. He was wrong. In the early 1960s, the Cuban government nationalized his business. He was again forced to flee, this time joining relatives in New York City.

Everyone who left Cuba because of the Revolution was forced to leave all possessions behind. My father was no exception. At the airport, on the way out of the country, a guard frisked him, found his battered watch, and asked him to remove it. He protested, "You've taken everything. Let me at least keep this." Surprisingly, the guard agreed. Years later, my father would give the watch to me, his son, as a family heirloom.

My father prospered in New York City's Chinatown. Rather than opening "just another Chinese restaurant," he and other Cuban Chinese with similar experiences decided to innovate, leveraging their Cuban background into a New York City-centric culinary movement that became known as Chino-Latino, a fusion of Chinese and Latin food.

Today, my dad's restaurant welcomes customers to its Jackson Heights, New York location operated by me, his son.

Asked about his thoughts on emigrating to the United States after twice escaping communism, my dad always says, "I'm grateful to be able to develop a business with the knowledge that it won't be taken away from me."

2

My grandfather served thirteen years as a political prisoner. He was the journalist grandson of Irish immigrants, spoke English fluently, and read voraciously. His living room looked like a library. He had many friends both within and outside of Cuba and communicated with them frequently. As the political situation continued to deteriorate, my grandfather wrote articles questioning some of the directives the government was implementing. He also wrote letters to friends in the United States, complaining about ration cards and forced "voluntary" service.

One night, the *milicianos* (militia) took him away. He was accused of counter-revolutionary activities and sent to prison in

Camaguey province, halfway across the country, where it was very difficult to visit him. He completed his sentence and died shortly after, a broken man.

His wife, my grandmother, served three years in a political prison. Her crime was hoarding. She had managed to collect enough little bars of soap to resell some at a small profit. This was considered theft by the government.

So many lives were destroyed in the attempt to simply survive.

3

I left Cuba when I was just twenty. I was engaged to be married to a young man I knew was enthusiastic about the Revolution. In contrast, I was totally apolitical.

My family had a pharmacy, and my mom had inherited property in Havana and Pinar del Rio, so we were well-off financially, if not wealthy. I was studying in the United States and looking forward to graduation and marriage.

During a school vacation, I went home to Havana to visit my family and my fiancé, Rafael. I remember Rafael would praise Fidel Castro and Che Guevara and the plans they said would lift all Cubans from poverty and create a new man, *el hombre nuevo*. I would nod enthusiastically and pretend to agree. He could have been talking about alien abductions; I didn't care. I just wanted to be with him.

After Castro came to power, things changed rapidly. Schools were closed, and businesses were nationalized. Rafael was ecstatic and rushed to join the *milicianos*. I returned to the U.S. to finish school.

My family became more and more nervous about the future.

Increasingly at odds with the political situation and in fear for their safety, my family decided to leave. They made plans to transfer money out of Cuba and into accounts in the U.S., where my aunt already lived, having emigrated there years before.

My mother was the backbone of our family. I remember her telling me not to tell Rafael about our plans. She believed the family should go to the United States and establish a life there. As the situation in Cuba continued to deteriorate, she believed Rafael would ultimately become disillusioned with Castro and follow us to the U.S. where we would be married.

I determined to follow my mother's instructions, but my resolve melted away one day when I spoke to him on one of our regular phone calls. I told him our plans and begged him to come with us. To alleviate any apprehension he may have felt about emigrating to a new country with no financial cushion, I told him about my family's plans to transfer substantial funds out of the country. He agreed to come with us.

The next day I received a call from one of our neighbors who told me *milicianos* appeared at our home and took my parents away. I learned my father was taken to *La Cabaña* (the notorious prison in Havana). He was accused of counter-revolutionary activities and given ten years in jail. My mother was accused of the same thing and given five years.

When my father finished his term, he was given an additional ten more years because one of his cellmates reported to the warden that my father had spoken against Castro. Nobody could be trusted.

Altogether, he spent twenty years in prison. When he was released, he was basically a skeleton with a skin disease that covered his entire body. I managed to get him out of Cuba and into the United States, where he died within the year. Other family members also left around that same time.

My mother died in prison shortly before her term was up. She was stabbed in the neck with a sharpened fork in an argument over a plate of food. This is what a former prisoner told me after she was released. This same prisoner asked me for money in return for information about my mother's death. I paid her $2,000 for that information. Even that small, sad piece of closure came with a price.

I went twenty years without seeing my family. Now I am eighty years old. I live with the knowledge that my young girl foolishness unwittingly condemned my family. I ask you to imagine living with that.

And Rafael? He rose in the ranks of the Revolution until a *chivato* (snitch) betrayed him, too. The *chivato* reported to his superiors that Rafael was involved in some plan to divert food from a distribution center to black market wholesalers that would resell at a high profit. Rafael, too, went to prison, and I lost track of him.

4

My grandfather was a military police officer. He worked prior to and during the Batista regime and was retired from the military by the time Castro took over. He abhorred communism and dictatorships.

He told a story about when he was ordered to interrogate prisoners. When in the room with the prisoner, he told them to scream, and he made loud noises to give the impression to anyone listening that he was beating the prisoners. He refused to torture anyone. One of the prisoners he had shown compassion to was a law clerk from my grandfather's hometown of Trinidad.

Years later, my grandfather was arrested for the crime of cultivating pineapples for personal consumption on his family's land in Trinidad without the permission of the Revolution. There was a family ahead of my grandfather whose crime was slaughtering their own pig to be sold on the black market. The entire family of five was sent to jail with a twenty-year sentence.

In the courtroom that day was that same clerk my grandfather refused to torture. The clerk vouched for my grandfather and convinced the judge to set him free.

A few years later, my mom quit her job at the telecommunications office in Santa Clara, Cuba before coming to the States. As she was preparing to leave, the *milicianos* came to pick her up and said she owed time to the *Agricultura* (farm work). She spent close to a year there working in horrible conditions and became extremely ill.

My grandfather sent a doctor to examine my mother because he also wanted the doctor to verify that she was unable to work in the hope they would let her go. Shortly thereafter, she was set free. She was emaciated down to eighty-nine pounds when she got out.

Meanwhile, the documentation to leave Cuba continued to wind its way through the system. Within another month or two, my mother was on a freedom flight to the United States in October 1968. She had nightmares about the experience for many years thereafter.

5

Right after the Bay of Pigs invasion, the situation was very tense. We lived in Matanzas and would go to Havana on weekends to stay with family. When we returned home to Matanzas right after the Bay of Pigs, we found the house *sellada* (sealed). Our neighbor said we had to go to the G2 office (office of the secret political police) to straighten the situation out.

I was a child and went with my father because my mother thought they were less likely to abuse a man with a small child. At the G2, we saw men who had obviously been beaten. They asked my father a few questions. Finally, they let us go, and two *milicianos* escorted us back home.

At home, we saw that they had ransacked the place, stolen valuables, and broken furniture. My father worked for a U.S. battery company as a regional salesman. During the search, they found some of the testing devices he used to test battery strength. They didn't know what the device was, so they accused him of using it to communicate with the enemy. After my father's explanations and some extremely uncomfortable moments, they dropped it.

Later that day, my father had to go somewhere. As he was backing the car out into the street, he saw the *milicianos* had spread the blood-stained uniforms of the *Brigada* 2506 (Cuban exiles who landed in the Bay of Pigs and attempted to overthrow Castro) in the driveway. I saw my father get out of the car and ask the *milicianos* to remove them. I don't remember what happened next, but I do remember the tense moments and the faces of my family.

6

One of my neighbors and her family tried to escape in a boat with fourteen other people. They were missing at sea for seven days with little food or water. Her brother could not deal with the dismal situation and not knowing if they would be rescued. He tried to jump off the boat as his sister tried to restrain him. He was too strong for her, pushed her away, and jumped off the boat. He drowned calling for his mother.

Finally, a boat found the remaining survivors. They were brought to Jamaica, and from there, they were sent back to Cuba where they were incarcerated. My neighbor was released after a year and sent to cut sugar cane in a "voluntary" program. Her relatives in the United States continued to push the process to get her and the remaining relatives out. After four years of hardship and uncertainty, they were able to leave.

7

Built in 1886, the legendary Perla Hotel was the original luxury Havana hotel. Over the years, it deteriorated like most buildings in Havana and became almost uninhabitable. An elderly woman lived there for many years, one of only a few remaining tenants. The story of how she ended up living there has a Shakespearean twist.

In 1961, the woman and her husband received permission to leave Cuba as exiles. As with all prospective exiles, their home was confiscated and nationalized. The couple didn't care what happened to their home as they were leaving anyway. At the airport on their departure day, they were told their visas hadn't gone through, and they were sent back to Havana. But now they had no home to return to, so they went to the Perla Hotel.

Weeks passed, and their visas never materialized. In frustration, the husband ingested rat poison and jumped from the balcony to his death. When the woman saw this, she too jumped but survived with broken legs and was returned to her room at the Perla.

Shortly thereafter, as a result of the communist party's property distribution project, the woman was allocated the hotel room to live in indefinitely. She remained there, cared for by some compassionate citizens, until her death. She was the last resident of the legendary Perla Hotel.

8

My mother left Cuba in 1953, long before the trauma of the Revolution, and settled in New York City.

When Cubans started to leave after Castro took over, they were forced to leave all valuables behind. My mother went back and forth to Cuba a couple of times, smuggling valuables for Cubans who had to leave jewelry and money behind. She would get a percentage of the value.

On one flight, just before takeoff, several people were taken off the plane for questioning. She was terrified they would call her and do a more thorough search.

Just before she left New York the second time to go to Cuba, my father told my mother not to go on these dangerous assignments. She responded, "Don't worry. If Fidel is in power by the end of the year, I'll be very surprised." Fifty years after that conversation, Fidel was still in power.

Just a little bit of bad luck and my mother would have been in prison forever—or worse!

9

My partner and I had already been living in the United States for some time when Castro came to power. I was an actor with a good reputation in Cuba, but I left because I wanted to develop my acting career in the larger U.S. Hispanic market.

After Castro came to power, I heard they were developing the performing arts in Cuba, and there would be many roles for actors. I returned and did everything possible to get parts in the theater or on TV but was not successful.

Slowly, I began to notice the discrimination against gay people like myself. One day, the G2 (Cuban secret police) came and told me I owed the Revolution work, and I was taken to the UMAP (Military Unit to Aid Production—forced labor camps where dissidents and homosexuals were taken) to cut sugar cane. I spent several months there.

I became very sick. As I was of no use to the government anymore, I was released.

My partner and I then began to do everything possible to get out because we were afraid of what the government could do next.

We finally managed to get out through Spain, like so many other Cuban refugees.

We were crushed, destitute, scared, and sick.

When we landed at the airport in Madrid, there was a representative of the Spanish government there, a short, stocky young woman. She was responsible for assisting Cuban refugees upon their arrival. She saw the sad state we were in and told us, *"¡Quiten esas caras largas! ¡Estan en su casa!"* (Get rid of those long faces. You're home now!)

We never forgot that wonderful reception after such horrible ordeals.

10

My mother brought a gold chain out of Cuba with her, hidden in her vagina. At the airport when they searched her, they made her spread her legs and jump up and down to release anything inside her. Luckily, the chain did not fall out.

We sold it after we arrived and used the money for necessities. She never told my father that she was carrying the chain inside her until after they were safely in the United States.

Such humiliation!

11

This year I will be celebrating fifty-three years since my departure from Cuba. On September 5, 1966, when I was fourteen years of age, my parents made the exceedingly difficult decision that thousands of Cuban parents had to make during those early years of the Revolution. They sent their children abroad, alone, in a desperate effort to get them out of the turbulent events that had taken hold of our country. Time was of the essence. I was only a few weeks from my fifteenth birthday, the age at which young men were no longer allowed to leave the country.

In my case, I was sent to Spain. My mother used to tell me that making that decision was very difficult for them, but ultimately it was the right decision. After she died, I found several things she had saved. I found a document called a *Patria Potestad* (parental rights) document, which declared me independent at the age of fourteen with the right to leave the country. I also found a small notebook they had made for me to put in my pocket before I entered the "fishbowl," that very hot enclosure at the Havana airport that separated families from each side of the glass. I believe that enclosure was made with the aim of increasing the pain of separation. For me, this notebook was an amulet or special pass that would help me on this trip that had no concrete destination. This notebook had the names and addresses of relatives in New York as well as the names of people to whom I could go for assistance in Spain.

Thank God that when I arrived in Madrid, I had the good fortune of finding people from my hometown of Holguin as well as other Cubans who helped me survive those early difficult days. Among them was a man who had gone to the shelter where I'd been taken from the airport after my arrival. He went there to help any of the arriving Cubans who needed assistance, especially the large number of unaccompanied minors who were arriving in Spain in those days.

He took me to where he was staying with his wife and two sons very near to the Atocha train station in Madrid. There he set me up in a room with the money I'd received at the refugee welcoming center, which was enough to pay for one month of lodging.

That first night, his wife prepared a meal for me like I had not seen in several years. Unfortunately, and with great embarrassment after one or two bites, I was not able to eat that meal. The pain of having left my family behind was too fresh in my mind. I missed my parents terribly.

That evening, and for the first few nights, I cried myself to sleep. The longing for my parents was very intense.

When I returned to Spain in 2015, the first thing I did was find my way to that apartment. The emotions were so strong, I simply stood there crying like a child, just like I'd done forty-nine years earlier, but this time I had the comfort of my wife's embrace.

Madrid was a marvelous place. Having arrived from a country that was quickly sinking into the dark ages, I felt the exuberance of someone who had just been given his freedom back, even though I missed my parents tremendously. It was bittersweet for me.

The first morning I was there, I went to a cafe in the Atocha station, very close to where I was staying. There I discovered a marvelous food called *churros,* fried dough you eat with chocolate. After a brief conversation with a young man who worked there who quickly realized the culture shock I was experiencing, we became friends.

From that day on, I had breakfast practically free every morning. I would pay him, and he would return most of the money to me as change. In the evenings, I would eat at a refugee center. There I had bean soup and a piece of bread, for which I will always be grateful to that great nation.

When I began to receive help from relatives who had migrated to New York City earlier, I was able to improve my diet. I ate a *choripan* (chorizo sandwich) and occasionally the classic "Cuban dish" of a fried egg over white rice, a banana, and a glass of wine for a few pesetas.

A few days after my arrival, the man who had helped me during those first few hours of my arrival in Madrid decided I needed shoes. The shoes I was wearing were of great sentimental value to me. However, they were already falling apart.

Those disintegrating shoes had originally been given to me by my uncle. As I was about to leave for Havana airport for my trip to Spain, my uncle noticed that the shoes I was wearing were somewhat dilapidated. He was wearing shoes that were just a bit more presentable than mine. He removed his shoes and gave them to me—his best shoes!

Years later, this uncle came to visit my family in the United States. The first thing I did was to take him to the nearest Florsheim

Shoe Store and buy him the most expensive shoes I could find!

But that day in Madrid, my benefactor took me to buy shoes in one of the very elegant shoe stores on the Gran Via. He bought me a pair of beautiful shoes. Unfortunately, when we got home, we realized the two shoes were of different sizes. As much as I tried to get my foot in one of the shoes, I could not; one shoe was much smaller than the other.

The next day we returned to the store, but the man in charge refused to fix the situation and would not take the shoes back. William told the man "Very well!" We then proceeded to stand in front of the store and show every person who came to buy shoes there what this man had done to us. After a while, the man came out and exchanged my shoes.

In Madrid, I met a young Cuban man who was also in transit with his family. Several years later, we found each other again at the same high school in New Jersey, and to this day, we remain good friends.

Later, I had the good fortune of joining people who had been the neighbors and friends of my family in Cuba and who had arrived in Spain a few months earlier. They offered me and another young man from Holguin, who had also come to Spain alone, the opportunity to go and join them. They lived in a village called Prados de Pravia in Asturias.

The trip from Madrid to Asturias was an overnight train trip. Unfortunately, the only ticket I could afford did not include a seat. Every time I found an empty seat, the conductor would tell me to move. Eventually, I found a good spot on the floor at the end of the wagon. I placed my dilapidated Cuban suitcase on the floor and laid on top of it, able to get some sleep.

The following morning, I arrived in the small town of Prados de Pravia where our former neighbors from Cuba lived. There we spent unforgettable moments. The lady who took care of the house was very welcoming and friendly. She made us delicious meals with fresh ingredients that came from her vegetable garden.

There was a river near the house where we lived called the Sella River. One day, under the famous Roman bridge of that town, I dove into the water headfirst as I used to do in the Almendares River in my town in Cuba, not realizing the water of this river was the snowmelt from the Picos de Europa mountains. The shock of the freezing water was so strong I almost drowned.

All the kids in the house had chores to do. I remember when it was my turn to go get milk in a large milk pitcher, I had to climb a hill where the dairy cow was. The owner of the cow had her in a room inside his country home and right there he would milk his cow.

To me, Prados de Pravia was a wonderful town. The people, the weekly fairs, and the cave of the Virgin of Covadonga were great experiences. I am so thankful to that family who treated me like their own.

In October of that year, I was summoned to the American Embassy in Madrid. After being interviewed by the ambassador and other officials, I was told I would be placed on the next available charter plane to New York.

On September 12 of 1966, I arrived in New York City. I will never forget the view of the Statue of Liberty as the plane took a bow over the statue on our approach into JFK.

In New York, I was finally reunited with my grandparents with whom I lived for the next year. Eventually, I reunited with my parents and siblings who were able to fly out directly to Miami. A few months later, my brother would have turned fifteen, and thus would have been unable to leave Cuba.

My family then settled in Elizabeth, New Jersey where my uncle lived and had a store. Over the years, just like other immigrants had done before, many Cubans made their new homes in Elizabeth. This town is where I grew up, where I met and married my high school sweetheart, and where I had my children. Elizabeth is what I now consider my hometown, a place that holds a special place in my heart.

12

Shortly before we came to the States, my mom, a very smart and courageous woman, decided she would not allow circumstances to call the shots in her life. She alone would chart her destiny.

She knew we would soon be in a desperate economic situation, and she would need to contribute to the family's survival and prosperity. She decided she would need her typewriter.

At the time, women used a small suitcase we called a *neceser,* a hat-box size piece of luggage for toiletries and essentials. My mother decided to make a false bottom for the bag so she could put the typewriter under it. Knowing my father would be appalled, she didn't tell him her plan.

On the day of our journey, Mami loaded up her typewriter in the *neceser* and covered the false bottom with underwear and cosmetics. She carried the luggage while they waited in the long line and through the inspections. I can only imagine how she must have felt. At that time, taking anything out of Cuba that was not authorized was considered theft and counter revolutionary. All this time, my father had no idea what she was doing.

Once on the plane and after takeoff, she turned to my father and said, "I can't believe I just did that!"

"Did what? What are you talking about?" he asked, wanting to know. She told him what she had done, and just as she suspected, he was terribly upset.

"Are you out of your mind?" he yelled at her in the airplane. "Do you know what they would have done to us if they'd found out what you'd done?" he asked her. "They would have imprisoned us all or worse!"

Fortunately for us, no one suspected a thing. Everything ended well. We safely made it to Miami, typewriter and all.

My mother's courageously foolish plan, and that typewriter, were invaluable when we got to the United States.

Mami was a wonderful journalist. Once in the United States, she contacted Spanish language newspapers and sold her compelling stories, including the escape from Havana with the typewriter. Little by little, she made a name for herself not only in the Miami Cuban community, but in other south

Florida towns as well as in New York City. She did this after she finished working her primary job at a factory. Her freelance writing made all the difference as we assimilated into our new life in the United States.

My parents will always be my role models. That's what heroes are made of.

13

My father had been against Castro and was unable to leave with the rest of the family, which included my mom and my twin sisters.

My mother was pregnant with me and had to go to the consular office in Havana alone to get the visas for herself and my twin sisters. The office was getting ready to close, and they told my mom she had to return another day. As the flight was the very next day, she couldn't return. She pleaded with them to help her.

I guess they felt sorry for this distraught woman with the bulging belly in the hot office, and they gave her the visas. She left Cuba the following day with my sisters.

I was born in Tampa one month after my mom got out of Cuba. Not only did she now have the twins to deal with, she also had an infant. My father did not arrive in Tampa until the following month.

I can only imagine the stressful times my parents must have undergone under these circumstances.

14

We had two dogs and a cat we were forced to leave behind. My mom loved the cat, but my dad was fanatical about one of the dogs, which he'd named Rodolfo Gutierrez as a joke and called Rody. And the feeling was mutual. That dog followed my dad everywhere. Once we knew we were leaving, we gave the cat and one of the dogs away to relatives, but Rody was to have a different destiny.

My dad had begun the process of getting Rody out of Cuba and into the United States, but our papers came through before he could manage it. We were forced to leave without Rody.

From the United States, we continued the process of getting Rody out. A few months after we were in the States, my aunt, who was still in Cuba, told us Rody had died. She said, *"Se murió de tristeza,"* (he died of a broken heart). Who knows why he really died? He wasn't that old.

My father fell into a depression so deep, we had to have him treated, Between the exile and his precious Rody dying, it was just too much for him. he eventually recovered, but he was never the same again. A little piece of him died along with Rody. He never got another pet.

15

I was twelve, and like most of my friends in the neighborhood, I had been signed up to leave by myself as part of the Peter Pan program. The notification of our departure flight would arrive by telegram, and being children, nobody wanted to be the last one.

The lucky ones, myself included, would be claimed by family members who were already in the United States. My parents, who followed four months later, risked their lives by crossing the Florida Straits in an ill-equipped boat.

Some of my friends were sent to foster care or group homes run by the Catholic Church, and for some, it was years before they saw their parents again.

16

Before Castro, my father worked for the Cuban government and had the luxury of traveling to the United States due to his job in import/export. Because of this, he knew the negative things being said about the United States by the Revolutionary government were not true.

One night, *milicianos* came into our home, told my father he was now recruited for "voluntary military service,"—basically drafted—and they took him away.

My father and about a dozen other men were sent to military barracks. Some received military training and were forced to remain in trenches for extended periods of time without contact with their families. It was more like a prison since it was not voluntary at all.

When he was released, my father was asked by a man in one of those trenches to send a message to his mother that he was still alive. My father agreed to do so and told the man he would keep tabs on his mother, too, to make sure she was all right.

We left Cuba and arrived in Philadelphia, having flown Pan Am. My aunt had come over years before and was waiting with other family members who had also left Cuba in the '50s. We all packed into her apartment and lived with them for a time.

Years passed. One day I had an awfully bad allergy attack and almost stopped breathing. My father rushed me to the hospital, afraid I would die. To his enormous surprise, the attending physician was the same man he'd met in the trench, whose mother my dad had offered to look after. To his dying day, my dad said that this man saved my life.

My father always thought that he would return to Cuba. He was eighty-seven when he died and never really lost hope. Toward the end, he had Alzheimer's and actually believed he was in Cuba. We went along with his delusion and would tell him we were on our way to La Habana Vieja or El Vedado. This made him happy.

17

My parents barely escaped. Some of our relatives were shot.

My father was an attorney working for a bank. The government accused him of alerting American companies of the impending nationalization of assets. As a result, he lost his job. We later learned it was a neighbor who falsely reported this to the government. That *chivato* ended up with my father's job.

Those were the days when families and communities turned on each other to curry favor with the local authorities. These betrayals were vulgar and cheap: malign your neighbor and get a better job. Inform on your childhood friend and get an extra chicken. Communism debased our society.

18

When we left, I had to leave my dog, Gallito, a Doberman, behind. We left him with neighbors. I imagine that with everything that was going on, the last thing they wanted was to worry about a big dog. In less than three months, my dog died. I'll never forget him.

19

Our plane left Rancho Boyero Airport one January morning in 1961. I was only eleven.

Within a short time, we arrived in Miami to stay with some friends of my father's family. We stayed there for a few days, then we left for an uncle's house in a small town in northern Florida.

My uncle had left Havana many years earlier, and he was the town's dentist. We were luckier than most Cuban exiles because we had established relatives already living in the United States.

Lake City was a charming northern Florida town. My uncle's house was made of red brick, unlike any house I had seen before. It sat on a big lot surrounded by large live oaks with drooping Spanish moss hanging on the branches and lots of pecan trees.

Having put up my parents, my two younger sisters, and me, the house was kind of crowded. My uncle himself had four young children.

The change from living in Havana to living in this small southern town was a shock, though. It was also our first experience of a real winter.

Soon after, I and my second sister were put in the local school. My youngest sister, being only three years old, stayed home. We didn't speak much English. I had a hard time understanding what was going on in class, but the teachers were very patient and understanding. It probably helped that my uncle was the town dentist and had pulled many a sore tooth.

There were students of both sexes in class in my new public school. This was a new experience for me as I had come from an all-male Catholic private school in Havana. It was a pleasant shock, though. I soon had a crush on one of the girls in my class. I don't think she even noticed me as she had her eyes on the class jock. Most of my classmates were nice to me, but not all, this being redneck country and all.

I made a couple of friends there during my short stay in that school. Our biggest pastime was throwing rocks at a nearby quarry. Exciting stuff!

A few short months later, my parents and I left for Puerto Rico. My father had found a job there as an appliance salesman. After staying a few weeks in a motel in the "Condado" section of San Juan, we moved to a rented house in the suburbs. The move from Lake City to San Juan was another cultural shock. We were speaking Spanish with everyone again, and the way of life in San Juan was very similar to Cuba's with the significant exception that Puerto Rico was not a communist country.

I soon made several Puerto Rican friends in the neighborhood. There weren't many Cuban families in there yet, though that would change soon. Although we shared a common language, many words for things and colloquial expressions were different. Being young, I was able to quickly catch on, including speaking in the Puerto Rican singsong accent.

I was enrolled in a Catholic private school again, although luckily, this time it was a coed school. Soon, I had another crush on a classmate. Again, she paid no attention to me. Her boyfriend was the class jock. I decided then and there to join the school's baseball team.

I stayed in Puerto Rico for many years until I left school for college in North Carolina, where I stayed for six years. That was another cultural shock. I moved to Miami after graduation and have lived there ever since.

Talek Nantes

I think the biggest lesson I have learned in life is learning how to adapt. It has helped me to survive the many shocks I have experienced since then.

20

My family had a mixed-breed mutt named "Lindo." He hated anyone dressed in the green fatigues that the military wore. He would growl and bark, ready to tear them apart any time he saw any militiaman in uniform.

My family had to leave him behind when they left in 1970. We left him with neighbors who got scared of his vicious streak and gave him away to a guy who lived on a farm.

A few months after that, we learned that some soldiers had shot him when Lindo tried to attack them.

21

To us, our photographs from Cuba were treasures.

I was recently speaking to my aunt, a woman in her eighties. She was telling me how most of her photographs were lost in Cuba. She said that when the *milicianos* got into her house, the photographs were destroyed and thrown into the wind from her balcony that faced a river. She watched her precious photographs drift away.

What was the point of such gratuitous cruelty?

My mother took our photographs out of Cuba with her. With all the things we had to worry about, and with the limited number of belongings we were allowed to take with us, my mother chose to rescue our family photographs and her cookbook, *Cocina al Minuto* by Niza Villapol. My niece inherited that cookbook and continues our Cuban cooking traditions.

22

My father was a political prisoner during the Bay of Pigs. For years, he had worked for an American communications company in the airport.

The very first day of the invasion, he was picked up by the G2 and disappeared for a week. Eventually, we found him at one of the mansions in El Vedado around the Avenida de los Presidentes. Those mansions were used by the government to interrogate people viewed with suspicion.

During that time, people the government considered suspicious were taken to *La Cabaña* in the middle of the night for execution, so of course we were imagining all sorts of horrors. We were very lucky to have found my father safe and sound.

23

We came on a freedom flight on August 23, 1967, escaping communism with nothing but the clothes on our backs. We landed in Opa-locka, Florida, then were bused to the Freedom Tower. For some strange reason, one of the things I remember about that day is that a man in a uniform gave me licorice. I had never tasted anything like licorice and found it very strange.

I remember seeing a woman at the Freedom Tower crying hysterically. I asked my mother what was wrong, and she told me the woman's son was not allowed to leave with her because they found out he had altered his age on his documents to avoid military service. Her husband, who was supposed to be leaving with them, thus stayed behind with their son. She was now alone in a strange country with no money and no knowledge of English.

We ended up in Boston. We had many hard times for a long time, but we are so grateful to America for accepting us. I love this country with all my heart.

24

In February of 1967, my mom, sister, and grandfather traveled out of Cuba via Spain. We had to leave my father behind as he was a doctor, and at that time, doctors were not allowed to leave Cuba. After a brief stay in Oviedo, Asturias, we were able to enter the United States in late June of that same year.

We came to Miami and stayed until October, then relocated to Dallas, Texas, which became our home. Having to leave my father behind was traumatic for us. He lost hope of ever coming to the States, divorced my mom, and remarried.

My mother dealt with the pain by working two jobs and retreating to her room to make dried flower decorations as a hobby. She became depressed, and my sister and I couldn't really count on her.

Nevertheless, we moved forward and thrived. We both got a college education and retired from good jobs. My mom died eight years ago, and my dad, who finally made it to the States, died three years ago. By then, he had separated from his second wife.

The Revolution totally and unnecessarily disrupted our lives. I believe our family would have been able to stay united and happy if we had not been cast into this revolutionary whirlwind.

25

In 1971, the situation in Cuba continued to deteriorate. Fearing that things could only get worse, a small group of family members and friends decided to escape Cuba through the Guantanamo naval base. It was that or taking to the ocean on rafts. They had no clue how to do this or how dangerous it could be. Regardless, they made their way through the rugged landscape and managed to make it to the perimeter of the compound.

The U.S. military detained us all. But instead of returning us or denying us entry, they brought us over to a base in Homestead, Florida and had us register as exiles. They gave my family emergency food and clothing and treated my aunt and cousin for minor injuries. My father said he was surprised at the care the U.S. government gave to this rag-tag group of desperate people who didn't even speak English.

My family requested to be sent to Chicago, Illinois where my two uncles lived. They had already escaped on a raft a couple of years earlier. We lived in the Chicago area for five years, then relocated to Tampa, Florida.

I can only imagine what our lives would have been like had we remained in Cuba. I love the United States, and my intrepid family that made those tough decisions. I think of their sacrifices and daring escape and wonder if I would have the courage to do the same thing today.

26

We came here in 1960. An aunt and uncle helped my brothers and me get to the United States. My parents came a couple of months later.

Another aunt went back, assuming she could return immediately. In the airport, she was stopped due to an issue with her paperwork and prevented from getting on the plane. That was a major fear Cubans had when leaving the country—that they'd be stopped and returned at the airport, separated from their families. She got stuck in Cuba until 1969.

Our parents worked hard. Little by little, we prospered. Their work ethic was their legacy that allowed us to retire from successful careers in the law, accounting, engineering, teaching, retail, and hospitality sectors.

We appreciate the United States and carry our Cuban culture in our hearts.

27

When we left from Rancho Boyeros Airport, my five-year-old brother had a basketball with him. The *miliciano* took it away from my brother and said, "There are plenty of these where you are going."

Both my brother and I had gold chains around our necks. When they searched my brother, they removed his chain and took it. When my turn came, I hid my chain in my collar, which I shoved aside with my hands, to show the *miliciano* I had no chain. He failed to see the chain, and I got to keep it.

Upon arrival in the United States, my brother saw a soda machine and asked my father to buy him a Coke. My father didn't have the necessary five cents and couldn't buy it. He often told us that not being able to buy a soft drink for his son that day was one of the saddest moments of his life.

28

Mom's uncle was arrested during the Bay of Pigs. He was considered a threat because he had vacationed abroad. Can you imagine anything more ridiculous?

He was released and got the hell out of Cuba. They let him go because he was old. He helped my mom's family get out.

29

My mom came to the United States with her two elderly parents and twenty-five dollars. My dad came here alone with even less money at age eighteen. He was able to get out by having his friend alter his birth certificate, so he could prove he was not of military age.

They both immediately started working and went to college while doing so. My dad could not finish college in Cuba because he was a practicing Catholic and disagreed with the government.

Mom finished college at the top of her class, even though she had small children and a part-time job. They retired early and did a little traveling. I attribute our family's prosperity and success to the example my parents gave us.

30

We left Cuba in 1967 after our dad, a political prisoner in *La Cabaña*, was released.

Our mom is from Spain, so my family went to Spain, and we lived there for about a year in Madrid, then emigrated to California.

Like many Cubans in a strange but welcoming country, our parents sacrificed for their children. We have made our lives successful in this country and are thankful for our freedom.

31

While my sister and I were going through my father's things after he died, I found cassette tapes that he had recorded in the late 1960s.

When I started listening to the first one, I broke into tears because I wasn't prepared to hear my father's voice.

The thing that shocked me the most was that on the tape, my father said, "Maria, if you are listening to this, it's a letter from me to you about when we left Cuba." The cassette broke, and I could never hear the rest of it. I would give anything to hear that tape.

32

I came with my parents in 1984 when I was four years old. We came because my grandmother was already here and was able to claim us.

My grandmother was separated from her husband, my grandfather, for over fourteen years because some of their kids were forced to stay in Cuba to serve in the military. My grandfather stayed in Cuba with the teens that had to stay while grandma came to the U.S. first with the younger kids.

My grandfather, my parents, and I followed later. We went to live in Massachusetts with relatives who had been established there for some time. My dad first worked in factories, and my mom worked as a teacher's aide. Eventually, my dad got a job at the post office and worked hard at that job until he retired twenty-five years later.

My parents worked hard all their lives. I'm so grateful they were so brave to sacrifice for me and leave the country they loved to come to the United States for freedom and a better life.

What courage these people had to go to a country where they didn't know the language or the culture and to start all over again to give me a better chance.

33

My dad came to the United States in 1956 before the madness began in Cuba. He came by choice. His father had told him, "Stop partying your ass off and go to work here in Cuba, or here is $500, and you can go to New York."

My dad left Cuba and never regretted it. He was always glad he and his family never had to go through the trauma of the Cuban diaspora.

34

I've always made it a point to share my parents' story with my children and grandchildren because it was so powerful and frightening. I wanted them to know what was important in life.

My dad was a teacher in Cuba. When he saw that things were getting so ugly, he and the whole family decided to leave. They left in a group of four small boats with other families. One of these boats was captured and all the passengers, including the women, were brought back to Cuba and put in jail.

The women were threatened with torture so they would give up information on who had helped them escape. The *milicianos* told them the other boats had sunk, their families had drowned, and what children were left were being taken to Bulgaria to be indoctrinated in communism. They were eventually released, and we later lost track of them.

After three days in the burning sun and freezing nights on the open ocean, the other three boats finally made it to the Florida Keys, where they were picked up by the Coast Guard. My mother was on one of those boats.

A few months after this ordeal, my father, accompanied by other survivors whose families were left behind, sailed to Cuba on a rented boat to bring the remaining relatives out of Cuba and into the United States. Several miles from Cuba, the boat sank. The passengers drifted in the ocean as they struggled to get closer and closer to the shore. They all made it except one man. This was the man who had been instrumental in negotiating the rental of the boat and had financed the rescue. Now they had to stay in Cuba until they could organize a new boat and another escape.

The group hid in different homes throughout Matanzas while they planned the escape that would finally reunite the families and get them all out of Cuba.

After several terrifying weeks, they managed to escape again. This time, they made it. Finally, the family was reunited. I was born shortly after that escape.

My regret is that so many of my family members died before their dream of a free Cuba was realized.

As I read through this yet again, it seems almost inconceivable that people were subjected to such extraordinary situations.

35

My uncle left Santiago de Cuba where he was stationed as a commanding officer of the local brigade because Castro's people were trying to have him executed.

He had to find a way to make it all the way across the island. He and his family hid in houses all along the route during the daytime and traveled at night until he reached the home of his communist brother in Matanzas.

Even though his brother did not agree with my uncle politically, family was family and he worked through a friend to get my uncle and his family asylum in the Ecuadorian Embassy.

They stayed in the embassy for several months, believing every day could be the day they would be arrested. Finally, they managed to leave through Venezuela and made it to Ecuador.

In Ecuador, my uncle got a job with the Hershey Corporation, an American company. He had gone to an English language school in Cuba and could speak the language pretty well. He was thrilled to get the job with Hershey.

After about three years in Ecuador, he asked for a transfer to the United States and was happy to get it on the first try. Shortly after arriving in the U.S., he made it his fanatical objective to get everyone who was left in Cuba out.

My family was among those that my uncle managed to get out of Cuba. We went to live with him and his family for about a year in very cold Rochester, New York until my parents got jobs, and we moved on to South Carolina.

This is a typical story of the round-about ways Cubans ended up in the United States.

36

It was a tremendous shock for us to leave Cuba. We left behind my father's entire family. I lost all my friends I had grown up with.

Over the years, I've forgotten much of what happened during those turbulent times. I think one of the reasons I've forgotten is a defense mechanism to protect me from the emotional pain of such a traumatic event.

I never saw my dad's family again. They all died, one by one. I never returned to the city of Cienfuegos where we were born; neither did my parents or any other family members.

Fortunately, I've found an old friend from Cienfuegos who left Cuba about the same time as I did and is now living in Orlando. We have reconnected. I've started to reminisce and remember people, places, and events through our long conversations.

Our family's story is just like most others. My grandparents and parents were middle-class working people, not rich, but not poor. My grandparents and my dad had a drug store in the center of town.

Like many others, we arrived in the United States and had to start from zero. We grew up in North Carolina, moved to Massachusetts in 1969, and settled in Kissimmee, Florida in 1989. We love this country as our own and love our Cuba, too.

37

The first three years after the communists took over, people in our country experienced a mix of feelings: sadness, fear, and, of course, uncertainty. I was just thirteen years old, and I remember my parents talking excitedly when we received our visa waivers (permission) to leave the island. Most of my family had already left.

That year the relations between Cuba and the United States ended horribly. As a result, the direct flights that had been everyone's hope were cancelled. We were now forced to begin the process of leaving Cuba all over again.

One day, a *miliciano* came to my house and told us I had to go to the local government office. A long-time neighbor, head of the *Comite de Defensa* (Committee for the Defense of the Revolution, CDR, a neighborhood watch group), had reported to the government that I was neither working nor going to school. Our local school was closed, so it's not like I had any choice.

The CDR had turned into a group of snitches who spied on and betrayed their fellow Cubans in hopes of gaining some favor from the authorities.

The *milicianos* didn't tell me to go to school. Instead, they sent me to work in the fields sorting pineapples and cutting sugar cane. The sixteen months I spent in the fields were the worst of my life. Finally, we were able to gather all the necessary documents, and the day came when we left Cuba forever.

Although it was a hard experience for me, those events prepared me for the life I encountered in the United States.

Once in the U.S., we were all reunited. We all started working and/or going to school at night to learn English immediately. For the next two years, I studied at night to get my high school degree. Then I went to college at night while working full time during the day.

We all made our successful lives in the U.S. I always tell my kids that the United States is the greatest country in the world and to run away from anything with even a whiff of socialism or communism.

38

I left Cuba in 1971. I was fourteen. They were sending young people at that age to labor camps. At age thirteen, I went to *La Escuela del Campo* (School in the Field), a sort of combination school and farm-work program. I was the youngest one in the entire camp. I missed my mother so much that I cried for a whole week. Fortunately for me, I wasn't there for too long.

39

It took us about ten years to leave Cuba. My father was sent first to the UMAP as a doctor. Then, he was sent to Batabanó where he ran the *policlinico* (outpatient center) as punishment for wanting to leave.

He told us that one day when he was working in UMAP, a man brought a patient to him with a machete gash in his foot. The machete had almost gone through the entire front part of the foot, which was hanging by some skin and ligaments. The man was screaming in pain.

There was no other option but to amputate the man's foot, but they didn't have the necessary equipment. They drove my father and the man to the nearest big town with a substantial medical department.

My father told me that the man's foot only needed to be partially amputated, but the only prosthetic the medical department had was one for a foot from the ankle down. So, they amputated the man's foot from the ankle, unnecessarily, just so the only available prosthetic would fit!

40

When my family presented exit documents to the government to come to the United States, both my parents were fired from their jobs.

They sent my father to Cienfuegos to cut sugar cane. Things were so bad he told us he even had to eat mice and orange rinds. Mom and I used to wash and iron clothes for a few cents. We sold things on the black market at night.

We had to endure insults and name calling at school. Even the teachers used to tell the other kids I was a *gusano* (literally translated as "worm" but actually meaning Cubans who wanted to leave the country). Once, in frustration, I yelled back at them that I might be a *gusano* but I was going to the United States while they were going to hell. That was a stupid thing to say in such a delicate situation, but I was so angry. I could tell by the faces of the people tormenting me that they themselves wished they were also going to the United States.

We finally got to the United States after six years of grief and uncertainty. The wait was worth it. We were free!

41

We arrived via the freedom flights in late 1966. By then, my grandfather and a cousin had been assassinated at *el paredón* (the firing squad). My parents had long ago lost their jobs and the food ration book and had been living off my uncle's generosity.

We arrived in Miami with one bag of clothing for two adults and two little girls. Only my mother could speak English, which she'd learned in college.

The refugee assistance program in the United States helped us find a place to live. They put the four of us in a little one-room efficiency apartment in Miami Beach. Rather than a full kitchen, we had a mini-refrigerator and a hot plate. These units were meant as temporary beach apartments for tourists who would spend a week at the beach. Now they'd been transformed into housing for Cuban refugees with entire families and all their belongings packed into one room.

The assistance program also gave us boxes of food. We received big cans of peanut butter, large bars of processed cheese, powdered milk, and eggs. You'd be surprised how good these things taste when you are hungry.

My mother, who'd been a stay-at-home mom in Cuba, found a job as a receptionist in a real estate office because of her English and go-getter attitude. Dad, who worked in a bank on Neptuno in Centro Havana, initially worked in a warehouse loading boxes. He studied English at night and eventually got a job as a teller at Sunbank.

We went to school and adjusted as well as can be expected after those bewildering first few days.

A few years later, we were able to bring my maternal grandparents out of Cuba. By then, we were renting a two-bedroom apartment, and although tight, we had room.

Once in the United States, my grandparents received the SSI, a small stipend from the U.S. government for elderly residents. They had never contributed to the U.S. economy, yet their final years were made that much more comfortable by the generosity of the United States.

I won't ever forget what the United States did for us and what the Cuban government did to us.

42

One of the most painful exile experiences for me was leaving my dog, Motica, behind in Cienfuegos. We were inseparable. I remember my parents told me my cousin would take good care of her, and we'd be reunited someday.

I remember talking to Motica and telling her that she was the only one who understood me. She would look at me with an expression that told me I was right: she did understand!

It's been over fifty-three years, and I still miss that precious little friend with her big brown eyes.

43

We came in December of 1965 through the freedom flights with my mom. She had been jailed for about a year for buying false documents as she was desperate to get to the United States where my father was waiting for us.

The documents she bought were poorly made and easily identified as false by anyone with any training. My mother told me she had paid for the documents with a couple of chickens. To what depths we had descended that we were trading poultry for false documents! What bizarre, unfathomable world was this?

Our family had been separated for almost two years.

It is not good to look back, but you shouldn't forget either.

44

We arrived in the summer of 1962 on a freedom flight with just the clothes on our backs. My dad almost didn't make it out because of an error in his paperwork. His two last names had been switched. An armed *miliciano* took my parents to an interrogation room. There they were told that my father would have to stay in Cuba and that they could either choose to stay with him or leave separately. They were terrified.

We were fortunate that a compassionate person in the airport was able to correct the error in time, and we were all able to leave.

I think these painful scenes that played out in the Cuban airports with people wanting to leave were a deliberate attempt to terrorize people who did not agree with the

Revolution. At least we got out. So many others did not.

For many months, nine of us lived in the same tiny apartment. My dad's first job was mopping floors in a resort. When I think of what my family went through, our current difficulties are nothing.

Today, with hard work and persistence, my parents are retired. They raised two children who received advanced degrees, and now have a granddaughter who is a professional and proud of her Cuban heritage.

The United States is indeed the land of opportunity! I am forever grateful America is my home!

45

We arrived in 1962. My dad found a way out through Venezuela, and the rest of us went to Tampa. They delayed our flight and almost didn't let my mom depart because of errors made on her paperwork on the U.S. side. My uncle straightened it out.

We went to live with my uncle and his family. My father finally joined us, and we settled in New Jersey, where we remained. All did well, like most Cubans who came at that time.

I held two or three jobs to make ends meet while adjusting to a new life.

Although I would have preferred not to have gone through the trauma of exile, I am glad how our lives turned out in the United States. We feel we are an American family with Cuban heritage and customs.

46

On New Year's Eve in 1958, my parents decided to take me to my first "grown-up" New Year's Party at the mansion of the local Westinghouse appliance importer who lived in a beautiful section of town called Paraiso. I was so excited over this big occasion.

I had gotten all dressed up for the party with a light blue organza gown and a little tiara with tiny pearls. The party was all I imagined it to be and I had a glorious time.

When the party was over, we headed back home and were shocked to see militiamen with machine guns blocking the entrance to our home! We were not allowed to enter our own home.

After some negotiations, they allowed us to go in, but they told us we could only take some of our personal property. "It's all our personal property!" my mother yelled. Then, they kicked us out into the street. They didn't let us back in, and they didn't let us take our car.

That was the beginning of our nightmare: January 1,1959, our introduction to communism. That happened to me, and I imagine it happened to so many others.

Since my father was the mayor of a city in Camaguey province before Castro's coup, and he never supported the new regime, all his properties were confiscated. He lost everything that he had worked for all his life, and we were basically homeless.

We managed to find a small apartment to rent. The *milicianos* came to our house again, broke the door down, ransacked the apartment, and took my father away. We wouldn't know for days whether he was dead or alive. A few days later, they released him and, not wanting to take any more chances, he went into hiding.

In April 1961, the U.S.-led Bay of Pigs invasion took place. As the news of the invasion spread throughout the country, the *milicianos* acted again. They came to the house and took my mother, my sister, and me. They detained us for nine days during the invasion because they couldn't find my father. He had been hiding for some time since he feared for his life.

My mother sent me to Havana, where my father was hiding. It was decided that my father and I should leave Cuba. We started all the paperwork to leave, which took almost a year.

Finally, the approval for me to leave came, but not my father's, so I left Cuba alone in January 1962 through the Peter Pan program. My father did leave a few months later. We were relieved that he got out and grateful he was not stopped.

When the Missile Crisis happened in October 1962, all flights out of Cuba were cancelled, so my mother and my sister were left behind.

During the Camarioca exodus, my father sent a boat to pick up my mother and sister, but they never managed to get on the boat. Finally, because I was a minor, my mother was able to leave Cuba in December 1965 with my sister through the freedom flights. Our family was finally reunited.

The nightmare odyssey had lasted seven years! So unnecessary. So pointless. All that suffering for nothing.

47

The *milicianos* entered our house countless times and stole our property. I was twelve years old and saw it all. My father had to escape because he had been in the military in the previous government. Six months later, we were reunited in Venezuela. A year and a half after that, we came to the United States.

I would like to return to Cuba to see where my family came from. I don't care if it is free or not. I just want to see it again before it is too late.

48

We were stuck during the October 1962 crisis. We had presented our papers in the police station in August, so we were waiting for the *salida* (exit authorization) to arrive any day. Those days became four long years. We didn't get out until October 1966.

49

My in-laws had a little food and fruit stand before Castro took it away from them. Their plan was to expand the stand into a restaurant. They worked that stand sixteen hours or more daily to *levantar cabeza* (get ahead financially).

My father-in-law was a Spaniard from Galilcia who emigrated to Cuba as an adult during the Spanish Civil War. He went to prison for no real reason, just as an excuse so the government could take away his stand. My mother-in-law was born in Cuba, the daughter of Eastern European Jews.

My husband's older brother was sent to Spain with his uncles to avoid the obligatory military. He died years later in the United States. He was never able to see his parents again. A sad story. The injustices that were committed against ordinary, hardworking people!

50

The Cuban government placed their supporters in charge of the nationalized businesses that they knew nothing about. The result was an economic disaster. Sadly, the government could not care less. Cuba's economic system was ruined. A healthy, vibrant economy was destroyed and was never able to recover.

51

My mother was born in Asturias, and my father in Galicia, Spain. They came to Cuba because of the Spanish Civil War. They met in Cuba and worked hard in their shop until Castro confiscated it. I was sixteen when they sent me to the United States to save me.

They arrived in the United States through Spain three years later. They both worked in our new country, my mother as a factory worker and my father as a bartender.

Thank God that because of them we are here!

I often wonder how different our lives would have been if the Revolution had not disrupted it.

52

Nos quitaron todo y si protestábamos, nos daban cárcel o paredón. A la familia de mi padre le quitaron las fincas en Trinidad.

A mi madre y primos les quitaron la finca tabacalera en Pinar del Rio. A nosotros nos quitaron la casa. La sellaron y nos botaron por querer salir.

A mi padre lo encarcelaron dos veces por pertenecer al ejército de Batista. Nunca olvidaré.

They took everything we had, and if we complained, we'd be put in jail or shot. They took my father's land in Trinidad.

They took my mother's and my cousin's tobacco farm in Pinar del Rio. They took our house. They sealed it and threw us out for wanting to leave the country.

They imprisoned my father twice for belonging to Batista's army. I will never forget.

53

My father left Caceres in western Spain for Cuba as a young man. Then, from Cuba, he went to the United States in the early '60s. His brothers didn't want to go to the U.S. because they didn't speak English. They preferred to go to another Latin American country where Spanish was spoken, and they could assimilate more easily.

After years of struggling to leave Cuba and escape communism, his brothers had a choice to go to either Uruguay or Venezuela. They opted for Venezuela.

Now that Venezuela has become a socialist state, the country cannot even feed itself! Venezuela had been one of the most prosperous countries in Latin America with a growing economy. Now my eighty-two-year-old father sends hundreds of dollars every month to his family in Venezuela just so they can eat properly.

54

January 1, 1959. That's when the Castro regime came to power and lives were disrupted forever. The Cubans from the exile generation that left in the early 1960s are inclined to divide their memories between life in the pre-Castro era and the period after that fateful date.

The very foundation of these Cuban's lives—businesses, life savings, homes, lifestyles, and freedoms—disappeared in a matter of months. Everything they had worked for...gone.

Entire families were shattered without justification or explanation. Some family members were allowed to leave Cuba while others were denied their freedom. To inflict even greater psychological terror on families, some members were taken off planes just before takeoff. Those family members who remained were left to wonder in anguish what became of their loved ones, when they would see them again, and if they could console a dying relative or return to bury their dead.

Life in the United States presented an equally daunting set of challenges, including how to survive. Doctors cleaned factory floors, lawyers and judges washed dishes and waited tables in restaurants, and university professors cleaned hotel rooms across the country.

Cuban women learned quickly that working outside the home would be the norm in the United States, especially if they wanted to prosper and not merely get by. They took what jobs they could and became factory workers, babysitters, maids, and the like to help their families. Even though they were starting from scratch in a new and unfamiliar country, the response to their situation was to move forward with discipline, perseverance, and an unmatched work ethic.

We all know that the example that generation presented was the basis of the success the next generation would enjoy.

It took more than mere persistence, discipline, and hard work for the exiled Cubans to prosper. What really helped them rebuild new lives and succeed was the assistance they provided to each other, that sense of responsibility for other exiles who were going through such difficult situations.

And it wasn't just family members assisting relatives. People frequently helped total strangers. Our neighbors took in a young couple with twins until they could get on their feet. My aunt cared for an elderly woman until her son found a job. Our family took in two teenaged siblings and provided them with a place to live and regular meals until their parents managed to get established with jobs and an apartment.

The community knew the dire situation people were in because they had lived it themselves.

55

We were two young Cuban girls arriving alone in Miami, Florida. We were positive about our future, but mostly scared, as we did not know if we would ever see our parents again.

Our parents were not allowed to leave because their documentation had errors. We had heard so many horror stories about families being separated, and we imagined this could also happen to us. A few weeks later, our parents were able to leave, and we were reunited in the United States.

We did okay after all, and we are thankful and humbled by the welcome and the opportunity that this great country has given us.

We are proud to be Americans. We look forward to many more years of contributing to the success and benefit of the United States and enjoying what it has to offer.

56

My husband was incarcerated because of his politics and was left behind in Cuba. I was pregnant at the time, but I did not know it.

Shortly thereafter, I realized my condition, which added to the stress of the upheaval. I was living with distant relatives who had helped me get out of Cuba. They did not anticipate dealing with a pregnant woman and an infant. Nevertheless, they were kind enough to help me with the birth of my son and then helped me take care of him.

My husband finally arrived two days before my son celebrated his first birthday. Of course, I would have preferred to have my husband to support me while I gave birth to our son. It was a very hard time in all our lives.

57

My husband arrived in Brooklyn on a Merchant Marine ship that left Cuba and had been sailing for three months.

He stayed in the United States with just ten dollars in his pocket because they wouldn't pay him until he returned to Cuba, and he didn't want to go back. That was sixty years ago.

I came later when I was ten with my dad. My mom and brother had to stay behind because my brother was already of military age.

My husband and I met in the U.S. and have been married for almost fifty years.

58

I boarded a Pan Am plane in Varadero, Cuba. My dad got held back with no explanation as he was about to board. That happened frequently in those days, and it terrified people. My dad screamed at my mother to get on the plane. She was hysterical.

I had never been on a plane before. I remember the ride being very quiet. Shortly after takeoff, the captain got on the loudspeaker and said, "Congratulations. You are now over international waters and out of Cuba's territorial air space."

Everybody cheered. A lone voice from the back of the plane started singing the Cuban national anthem. Little by little, other voices joined in until everyone was singing along while tears streamed down their cheeks.

I remember my first sight of Miami. It seemed enormous. I have no memories of the landing or leaving the plane. The next thing I remember was being given a ham and cheese sandwich with chocolate milk and a peach. I had never had chocolate milk before. It was heavenly. And that peach was so sweet and juicy!

I remember crowds of people, so many people everywhere. A big building. Lots of stairs. A doctor and a nurse.

My next memory was choosing a dress and shoes. Then I was given a little package with a brush, a toothbrush, and Colgate. I'd never tasted Colgate and really liked the taste.

I remember a long hallway and steps out of the building onto the sidewalk. Then nothing again until waking up the next day in a strange house with people talking and my mother's excited voice.

I was disoriented. I wasn't sure if I was dreaming. I didn't know where I was. I went looking for my mother and found a house full of people I didn't know. I was told they were cousins. A television was playing. There was a program on about a woman who twirled around in a voluminous skirt. My mother watched and occasionally would break down and cry hysterically. The people there tried to calm her down.

Our cousins made us something to eat and took us to a supermarket. The massive doors opened by themselves and cold air wafted toward us. I remember being overwhelmed and amazed at the sight of all the food. There were large sections of different kinds of meat, rows and rows of vegetables I didn't recognize, and boxes with cartoons on them. It was like a dream. I could never have imagined all the food I saw in that supermarket.

I asked what was allowed on the quota. My cousins said there was no quota and told me to pick whatever I wanted. I picked apples and hazelnuts. Then I recognized the peaches they had given me the day before and took two.

My cousin and my mom cried.

Two weeks later, my dad arrived, and we left for Texas.

I will never be able to thank this country enough. And we always have peaches in the house.

59

I remember we left via Rancho Boyero by air, and I recall when we arrived at a big building. The most difficult part was when we were separated from my father. For me, it seemed like many hours, but I really don't know how much time passed. When he returned, all he said was that all was well, and it was just an interrogation. We were free now.

60

I was fourteen when we arrived in the United States, and I was not allowed to wear lipstick. Among the things they gave us was a little tube of lipstick. I was dying to wear it. I remember the smell. Mom saw me looking at it and said I should try it to see what it looked like. What a surprise that she allowed it! After I put it on, I thought it looked too red and I removed it. The things we remember!

61

I don't know if it's good or bad that I remember every detail. I wrote down all my thoughts from the moment the plane took off until we landed in Miami.

I've saved those pieces of paper like treasure. What experiences, what sad adventures we Cubans have lived! Every exile has his own story.

62

The first time we tried to get out of Cuba was through Varadero. It was 1966. We were ready to go, but they wanted to keep my brother who was thirteen because he was too close to military age. My uncle suggested we get someone to alter my brother's birthdate on his paperwork, but my mom was too scared. She had heard stories about people who had tried to do this and ended up working as "volunteers" in the sugarcane fields. My parents wouldn't leave him behind, so we stayed.

Fortunately, our second attempt was successful, and we all got out.

The tension as we waited for takeoff was palpable. At first, it was very quiet as the plane was taking off. I kept hearing whispers of *gracias a Dios* (thank God), and *bendito sea Dios* (blessed be God). Shortly thereafter, there were lots of tears and clapping as the plane left the ground.

We were happy to have made it out but sad to be leaving our loved ones behind. In those years, we were told we could never return. In time, many of our relatives who got left behind died one by one, and our past lives in Cuba were slowly snuffed out like candles in the wind.

63

When my mother left in 1976 via Mexico, I didn't even recognize her after fifteen years of separation. She was sixty-six, skinny, and wearing a headscarf, a faded sundress, and rubber slippers. Her small cardboard suitcase had broken. I asked, "Are you Maria?" She answered with a hug.

I told her that first thing the next day we were going to buy her new clothes. She seemed like a little girl in a fantasy land when we went to a large department store named Palacio de Hierro. She touched everything, and she ate everything she could.

I remember her with love but also with sadness for having missed all those years when we could have been together. May you rest in peace, Mami.

64

We left Cuba in 1969. I was almost two years old, and my brother was almost three. I don't remember any of it. I've heard all the stories of our leaving Cuba.

My grandmother and mother said that when they landed in the United States, the people were so nice and welcoming. They gave my mom a delicious cup of hot chocolate. She said she will never forget this.

We are so thankful for everything this country has done for us. We thank God and America every day!

65

It is amazing how, after so many years, our memories are so vivid. I came on Christmas day in 1960, and I still feel the fear and the pain of separation.

My parents came in November 1962. It had been hard leaving them behind, but it was also hard getting to know them again. At first, we were awkward with each other. Everyone had changed, including us.

My parents are both gone now.

The story they always told me was that all the men were removed from the flight except my dad and a man two seats away.

 The remaining passengers sat on the tarmac for one agonizing hour, not knowing if the men were coming back or if the flight would leave. Then the pilot told the passengers that the men were not coming back, and anyone who wanted to get off and join them was free to do so. A group got off.

Once the flight took off, the pilot flew around the island and told the passengers to look out the window and take one last look at Cuba because who knew when we would see our homeland again. Sadly, that was the last sight of Cuba for many people.

66

My parents never shared the story of when they left Cuba. It was too painful.

Only after my father aged and began suffering from Alzheimer's did he start talking about it and saying he was going back. He insisted he was going to visit his parents who had died decades ago. He was never the same again.

67

I had to leave my dog, Chichi, behind. He was a poodle and cocker spaniel mix. I would dress him up in little hats, and we would sit on the terrace of our home to watch the people pass. Everyone made a big fuss over him. Just a couple of months after we left, we received news that he had died. We think he was poisoned. How cruel! Who would do that?

68

These stories are repeated many times with different situations. I do not get tired of hearing what my fellow Cubans experienced.

We are grateful to the country that opened its doors to us and allowed us to live in freedom.

Thank you! God bless America!

69

The one thing I wanted to bring to the United States when we were given "la visa waiver" was a blue and white toy sports car I got for Three Kings Day (a holiday in Cuba during the Christmas season, when children traditionally receive gifts). I had seen it in a store window in Matanzas and thought it was the greatest toy ever created. I had to have it. My dad said, "Let's see if the Three Kings will bring you one."

I was thrilled to see it waiting for me on

January 6th under our tiny Christmas tree along with a big doll for my sister. I remember my mother pointing to a little crack under the door of our yard and telling me the Three Kings and camels had shrunk enough to fit under the door.

Later, I learned that the Bulgarian-made toy had been the most popular toy in communist Cuba that year and had sold out. My parents had searched our entire province to find one for me.

On the night we arrived at the Varadero airport, in preparation for our next day's freedom flight to the United States, a uniformed *miliciana* with a menacing pistol at her side inspected our suitcases.

She asked to see my car, but I was terrified of losing it, so I hugged it and shook my head no.

My dad told me to let her see it. I complied. The woman took the toy and shook it so violently that it started to come apart. At the sight of my precious toy being destroyed, I started to scream. My father pleaded with the *miliciana* to stop destroying the car.

"Please, have compassion for the child," he said. He pointed to the bottom of the car which was transparent and impossible to hide anything. Surprisingly, the woman relented. She held the car up to the light and saw through the plastic that there was nothing in the toy. They let us move through with the toy car.

I did not let go of that car until after we arrived in Miami, and I still have it today. It is faded and peeling. The plastic is cracked and being held together by tape. It's a beautiful reminder of the sacrifices my family made, how they protected us during a dangerous and tumultuous time, and how I arrived in the United States clutching an important connection to my past.

70

I had a doll with blond hair that my aunt brought me from Spain in 1960. I left Cuba in 1967, and I wanted to bring my doll. When they took inventory before I left my house, they told me I was too big to play with dolls. I still remember what she looked like and her blue tulle dress. Who knows who has my little doll!

71

We all can remember moments before we left that could have changed our lives completely. What if that guard at the airport hadn't let you through, or our passports were denied?

Can you imagine how different our lives would have been?

72

We were only allowed one suitcase per person. Tia got us new clothes in Miami, and we burned what we wore on the boat. That was a foolish thing to do, but we felt we were breaking with the past. By that time, we'd had enough of Cuba and the craziness, fear, uncertainty, and suspicion that surrounded us.

We were thrilled to be in the United States. For years afterward, whenever someone mentioned Cuba, my mother would say, *"A mi no se me perdió nada en Cuba."* ("I never lost anything in Cuba," meaning I have no reason to go back to an unpleasant place.)

My mother made a success of her life and helped us to do likewise, and she never looked back.

73

To get out, we pretended that my father, a pharmacist, was "supposedly" attending a conference in Miami and taking my mom and me with him. My older sister had already left the island on one of the Peter Pan flights arranged by the Catholic Church. The church would soon be forced to leave Cuba, too, as the official doctrine of the country was now atheism.

The Cuban government limited the articles you could take, including clothing. They took my mother's wedding ring right off her finger. This was right before flights to the United States were totally shut down.

I remember my parent's sad faces and my grandparents crying as they saw us off. My mother pressed her hand against the glass where my grandmother was also pressing hers on the other side while they both cried.

My mom and I were strip searched. We knew my dad was going through the same process in the room next door. My mother was terrified that the small gold chains hidden in the hollowed-out lining of my father's suitcase would be discovered. To him, the chains were worth the risk because they ensured that we would not go hungry. We never sold the chains and still have them.

What kept us going was my parents' motivation and willingness to work hard. Also, their willingness to be humble, taking work unloading boxes in warehouses and working in factories. Those packages of food from the U.S. *refugio* (refugee center) also helped.

How many of us today with advanced degrees like my parents would set aside our pride and do manual labor? They did. And that made all the difference in our progress and success.

It is hard to fathom the courage it took for my parents to leave everything behind in Cuba and bring their young daughters to the land of freedom. Thank God they did!

74

Cuando llegamos al aeropuerto, mi hijo de cinco añitos empezó a llorar y le dio un ataque de asma. En el apuro de salir del país, no trajimos su medicina. Sin medicina tuvimos que regresar a la casa, pero ya estaba sellada. Tuvimos que dejar mi hijo en el hospital local hasta que localizamos medicina. Ya que no teníamos casa adonde regresar, nos quedamos en casa de una vecina. Nos tomó seis meses más para volver a intentar la salida que finalmente logramos. Eso fue en el año 1971.

At the airport, my five-year-old son began to cry and had an asthma attack. In the rush to leave the country, we had forgotten his medicine. Without his medicine, we had to return home, but the government had already sealed it. We left my son in a local hospital and went in search of his medicine. Since we had no home to return to, we stayed with a neighbor. It took six months more for us to make another attempt to leave, this time successfully. That was in 1971.

75

It's a pivotal scene that played out in the lives of so many Cuban exiles as they left their homeland. The communists took all our personal properties, spitting us out into the world with the clothes on our backs and the humiliation of body searches while being robbed of our few possessions.

76

We arrived on the Fourth of July. Every year thereafter, we're reminded of our arrival in the land of freedom.

77

I was seven when we left. I didn't want to leave. I had my friends and my toys. I was waiting for the Three Kings to bring me a wonderful toy I'd seen in a window. My parents told me we were only going on a temporary trip and would return soon. But others had told me that once we left, we would be gone forever. That concept was frightening. How long was "forever"?

When they were searching us, I told the *miliciano* that I was only going for a short time and would return soon. He laughed and said that Cuba didn't want *gusanos* (worms). I didn't know what he meant and started to argue that I was not a worm until my father pushed me forward.

It was not until we were safe on American soil that my father explained how "lucky" we had been. He had feared our trip would have been denied just before we boarded our flight to freedom!

I am glad to say that fifty-one years later, my sister and I are so happy to be in the United States.

78

When we left from the Havana airport in 1969, they took an entire suitcase from us. They said the suitcase was over the limit, and we would have to leave it behind. Unfortunately, part of that suitcase's contents were our family photos. My father began to plead with the *miliciano,* but Mom said, "Leave it. Let's just go."

Our precious photographs! My parents' wedding photos, my confirmation, family picnics with people I never saw again. Our family's photographic history, gone forever.

79

I had two beautiful pets, Blanquita, a white kitten, and a dog, Cuqui, a mix of Chihuahua and I don't know what else. I was eight, and I still remember taking Blanquita in a box to my aunt's house when we left. She would write to me afterward and tell me how Blanquita was doing and that she was growing nicely.

My dog, Cuqui, was poisoned by one of the *hijos de puta* (sons of bitches) from the CDR after I left at the end of 1961 because it was a *"gusano's* dog." They probably ate him.

PART 2 - STRUGGLES ON ARRIVAL

PART 2
STRUGGLES ON ARRIVAL

1

When my mother died in Miami, my sister and I went through her belongings. We found a little leather packet with something soft inside. We opened it and found sand with a little note that said, *"Tierra de mi Cuba"* (land from my Cuba). Had I known that existed, I would have buried it with her.

2

When she first arrived from Cuba to New York City, my mother worked in a factory that made stuffed animals. While there, she befriended a little Chinese man who would always follow her around. They would have lunch together and worked side by side on the assembly line. I don't know how they were such friends because my mother only spoke Spanish and the Chinese guy only spoke Cantonese.

One day they were both fired, supposedly for being too slow. They both left the factory dejected and went back to the employment agency to look for new jobs. At the agency, they were heartened to learn that two positions had just come on the market. They were so happy until they learned that they were the same two jobs they had just been fired from.

3

We first arrived in Flushing, New York and needed to find a place for the four of us— Mom, Dad, my brother, and me— to live, but we had almost no money. My father had just gotten a job. It paid very little but at least it was something.

We found a studio apartment for ninety dollars a month with the first month free if we signed a two-year lease. The only catch was that it was only for two people. We decided to take it anyway, and my brother and I spent the next two years sneaking in and out of our little studio apartment, so the super wouldn't see there were four tenants instead of two.

My parents stretched out a sheet in the middle of the room to separate themselves

from us. My brother and I couldn't afford beds, so we had two little army cots. They were cheap and fragile. Whenever we moved, they would flip over, and we'd land on the floor. We tried to sleep like stiff little corpses, but inevitably we'd move and again tumble onto the floor. Finally, we gave up and just made our beds on the floor until we saved enough to buy beds and get a bigger apartment.

These stories may sound humorous now, but they were nothing to laugh about at the time.

4

My family-run restaurant was a thriving business just outside Havana in the 1950s. My brothers and I built the restaurant with our bare hands from four wooden planks and a thatched roof to a vast operation including a dancefloor, playground, and event salon able to hold over two thousand guests.

The most popular celebrities of the day regularly frequented our restaurant. The restaurant was at its peak when the newly installed communist government expropriated it in 1962. Devastated but not defeated, we listened to a fellow entrepreneur who had left Cuba to reopen his butcher shop in New York City and decided to follow suit.

We emigrated to the United States and worked in factories for many years until we saved enough money to reopen our restaurant in 1976, this time in the U.S. By sticking to the same classic Cuban recipes and welcoming family atmosphere, we recreated our earlier success. Today, we have two successful restaurants in the New York City area.

5

My father, a sweet, gentle man, was born in a tiny village in Galicia, Spain. He didn't have much schooling and barely spoke Spanish, much less English.

Coming to the United States in 1965, his second emigration in a lifetime, was traumatic for him. He had difficulty with his speech. In the United States, he seemed to get worse and had trouble with both English and Spanish words. For example, instead of "empty," he'd say "guilty." Instead of "excuse me," he'd say "escupe." We thought he might be dyslexic, but nobody knew about those things back then.

He got a job at a Winn Dixie supermarket collecting shopping carts in the parking lot. His speech deteriorated to the point that he was barely comprehensible, and about five years after arriving, he died of a stroke.

We always believed that the second emigration was just too much for him and had he stayed in his peaceful, comfortable life in Cuba, his life would have had a different and much better ending.

6

My father and his brothers ran the family pineapple farm in Cuba.

My family had the foresight to recognize the coming adversity and terror of Cuba's new communist government. They sacrificed everything they had worked for in order to escape.

Aided by the Catholic Church and taking their four young children, my parents fled Cuba with only the clothes on their backs. They settled in Boston in 1968.

They quickly adapted to life in the United States despite the challenges. My father's work ethic drove him to work multiple jobs to support his family.

My parents eventually settled in Elizabeth, New Jersey with their four children. Both of my parents had lengthy careers with the Movado Watches Corporation.

Everything my parents did from the moment they arrived in the United States was for their children, so they could have a better life!

7

My parents were already in the States. The families had careers as musicians and educators in Cuba but had to give them up when they left. When Castro took over, they decided to remain in the United States and help most of their relatives escape.

My uncle couldn't make up his mind between leaving and staying. He was a bandleader/composer and owned a little club near El Cristo that was popular with Havana's artsy crowd. He lived a comfortable existence and was convinced the Americans would never allow a communist regime just ninety miles off their coast. "Castro will soon be overthrown," he insisted. He repeated that sentiment loudly and often.

Things changed quickly after Castro took power. The government nationalized my uncle's club with no compensation. They offered him the opportunity to work in his own club as an employee. He did this for about a month while he continued to speak ill of Castro to anyone who would listen.

One day, the *milicianos* came and accused him of counter-revolutionary activities. He had been betrayed by a *chivato* who was trying to ingratiate himself with the local authorities. They sent him to the UMAP where they usually sent gay people like my uncle. An artistic, sensitive *bon vivant* who had lived a life of music, fashion, and clubbing was suddenly forced to do hard labor in the sugarcane fields.

News of my uncle's dire circumstances reached his family in the States who mobilized to get him out, but by now, the process had become onerous and drawn out.

Time passed. My uncle found the labor unbearable, and one day, he sliced part of his foot off to avoid work in the sugarcane fields. In the local rudimentary hospital, he caught an infection.

He never left the hospital. He died there.

My family didn't know he had passed away and continued to process his paperwork. We didn't hear from him, and one day, a neighbor of my uncle contacted a relative in Miami who reached us in New York to tell us my uncle had passed.

We never found out where he was buried. A few days later, his papers came through to go to the United States.

8

I heard this story from an old friend. His dad came from Cuba in the early '60s and, desperate for a job, applied for a position as a mortuary assistant. He had gotten the job by telling the owners that he had many years of experience. In fact, he had never been in a mortuary in his life. He managed to do the job by watching what other employees did and imitating them.

After a few weeks of successfully pretending he knew what he was doing, he was trusted enough to be left alone on a job that needed to be completed overnight. His responsibility was to dress the embalmed corpse of an old woman and put makeup on her. He had an idea of what to do from watching the employees. With trepidation, he began his task, alone, at night.

He applied simple make-up on the corpse's face and managed to get a dress on her. Just as he was getting ready to deposit the corpse into the coffin, he heard a deep sigh. He knew he was alone, so he froze. He turned and saw the corpse's arm had fallen off her chest.

He immediately left and went home. All night, he debated whether to return to work the next day, but the desperate economic situation and the need to provide for his young family forced him back.

The next morning, he returned before anyone else and found the corpse in the same position. He forced himself to reposition the corpse and deposit it into the coffin.

Weeks later, he learned that sometimes air and gas get trapped in a corpse and is released when the corpse is moved. This explains the "sigh" and the movement of the arm.

He kept that job for almost a year until he found a better one and still calls that night the most terrifying of his life.

9

When we left Cuba, we had to leave my grandparents and dog, Rocky, behind. Four years later, it looked like my grandparents would finally be allowed to leave, but my grandfather refused to leave Cuba unless we got the dog out first. So, with everything else my struggling exiled family had to worry about in their transition to a new country, we decided to get the dog out of Cuba and into New York City.

My grandparents had heard that it was extremely cold in New York. They were concerned it would be too cold for the dog. My grandmother cut up the sofa upholstery and sewed a coat for Rocky. I don't know how we got him to the States, but I remember Rocky transferred through Bermuda.

It was just before Christmas when we were advised Rocky would be arriving at JFK. We gathered what little money we had and took a taxi to the airport. We were so excited and shared our story with the taxi driver. The driver was an Eastern European Jew. He said he, too, was driven from his country after WWII and had to emigrate to the United States. When we arrived, he refused to charge us for the fare.

When Rocky was let out of his carrier after  his long journey, he was so happy to see us he peed on all our shoes. We all cried and hugged him with his little blue and white sofa coat.

A few months later, my grandparents arrived in New York. Rocky lived a long and happy life. He and my grandfather died just a few days from each other.

10

Shortly after we arrived in Flushing, Queens, New York in 1962, I got a job as a paper boy to help at home. I had to distribute the now defunct *Long Island Star Journal* to customers throughout the neighborhood.

I was twelve and had to lug the papers  around very early in the mornings. All I had to do was leave the paper on the customer's doorstep and collect once a week.

There was this one customer, an older woman with hair dyed a color I'd never seen before, who would invite me in and give me hot cocoa. I remember breathing in the aroma of that delicious chocolaty brew, so appreciated on freezing winter mornings.

One day, the woman had a plate of Easter peeps waiting for me. These were little yellow marshmallow candies in the shape of baby chicks. She was wearing a flimsy negligee that was slightly opened in the front. I sat down to drink my cocoa and she moved closer to me, pushing the plate of peeps in my direction. As she leaned over, the negligee fell open, and I saw her exposed breasts very close to my face. The things that stick in our minds!

11

We had applied to leave through Venezuela and the United States, both places where we had relatives. We had decided to leave for the first country that gave us the famous "visa waiver," and Venezuela came through first.

After a few months in Venezuela, we were approved to enter the U.S. and initially settled in New Orleans, where I had an uncle.

Shortly after our arrival in the Big Easy, my father got a job, and we set off to the local supermarket to buy groceries.

Of course, we had very little money, so we had to budget carefully. We started off with twenty dollars, which went a long way in the early 1960s. Every time we bought something my father would deduct the price from the twenty dollars. We bought rice, beans, milk, weird soft white American bread that came in square slices, chicken hearts and gizzards, potatoes, and a strange concoction that had been recommended to us because it was cheap and filling called macaroni and cheese.

As the shopping cart filled up, the twenty-dollar budget continued to shrink. When we reached twenty dollars, my father yelled, "Stop!"

We each grabbed a bag and left with our groceries.

That "financial management" lesson stuck with me through life, and I've always lived within my means.

12

We had almost no furniture when we arrived in New York City. What little we had did double duty; the kitchen table was used as a workplace, so we could make necklaces in our spare time and get paid by the unit. The bathtub was also used as a place for washing clothes. When there was no water in the tub, we used it for storing clothes because we did not have a proper chest. We had beach chairs in the living room.

For several months, some of our family members took turns sleeping in the same bed. My uncle, who was staying with us, worked at night, so he slept in the bed during the day. My parents slept in the same bed during the night. Our little apartment was bare and sad. Furniture was something we coveted.

Talek Nantes

I remember walking the streets of Manhattan with my parents and being 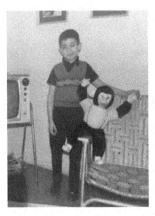 amazed at the things Americans threw out.

They would take items they no longer wanted and dump them on the sidewalk for the garbage truck to remove them. In our furniture-deprived eyes, many of the items were still good. There were night tables that just needed a good scrubbing, lamps that just had to be rewired, and loads of bookcases that just needed a reinforcing bracket.

We took these items home, carrying them through the summer heat or wintry cold, fixed them up and gave them a second life in our dingy apartment.

Little by little, we got our heads above water and moved into better accommodations, leaving that garbage-picking life behind.

Some experiences brand you for life, though. Even today, sixty years later, I'll look at a discarded piece of furniture on the sidewalk and think "hmmm ...."

13

When we left Cuba, we were only allowed to take one extra set of clothes. To top it off, we arrived in New Jersey in October with no winter clothes, so we knew we had to get warm clothing quickly or we'd freeze.

We learned from the Cuban grapevine that there was a charity thrift shop that gave away clothing to recently arrived refugees. Indeed, the thrift shop had clothing, but it was the most bizarre collection of discarded garments imaginable—Russian-style aviator caps with earmuffs, fancy hats with plastic flowers like the hats old ladies wear for church on Sundays, floor-length embroidered oriental robes, leopard-print leggings, and the like. These were more like costumes than regular street clothes. Still, they were free, and some were warm, so we grabbed a few.

I ended up with a green, double-breasted coat that was at least two sizes too big for me. It had epaulets, silver buttons, huge lapels, and it was so long it reached almost to my ankles. That coat had never been fashionable. It must have been a factory reject that somehow ended up in the thrift shop. Still, the coat and a wool cap were better than nothing.

Now I needed shoes. I found a pair that, although several sizes bigger than what I needed, were not as fashionably objectionable as my coat and looked warm. I took the shoes, and my mother packed the tips with newspaper so they would fit better.

At the first snowfall, my shoes got soaked, and the newspaper-filled tips got wet and began to curl upward, so they looked like Aladdin or fairy shoes. The combination of that ridiculous coat and the curly-toed Aladdin shoes was deadly for a teenager with hopes of maybe impressing a girl.

But it doesn't end there.

When we first arrived in the United States, it was all-hands-on-deck. Everyone had to go out and earn money for the family. My father got a job as a bookkeeper, my mother went to work in a factory making plastic Batman glasses—Batman was all the rage back then—and I was a paperboy.

To earn extra money, my mother bought a bunch of plastic Batman glasses at a wholesale price from her factory. She furnished a little box with a string that I hung around my neck and filled it with the Batman glasses. Then she sent me out to sell the glasses in front of the subway station.

Every day after school that winter, I stood in front of the subway with my army coat and Aladdin shoes, hawking plastic Batman glasses to bemused commuters that emerged from the subway.

14

When my mother first arrived in New York City from Cuba, she got a job as a maid in Ronkonkoma, Long Island. We used to make fun of the word "Ronkonkoma" because it sounded so funny.

One day, the owner of the house, a Jewish woman, left to go shopping and told my mother she'd be back in a couple of hours.

My mother took this opportunity to make herself a sandwich of lox, something she had never seen before arriving at the woman's house. She loved the salty taste of that fatty fish. She piled the lox on and added all the ingredients she had seen the woman add.

Just as she was biting into the sandwich, the woman returned because she had forgotten something and saw my mother with a mouthful of lox. My mother was mortified, believing her employer would think she was abusing her hospitality. The woman looked at my mother, said, "Enjoy your meal," then left, and never mentioned it.

My mother always told me that woman had a lot of class.

15

I came to the United States with my cousin, Carlos. The only people we knew in the U.S. were distant relatives who lived in New York City. They had told us it was easier to get jobs in New York and that the jobs paid better than in Miami. We didn't have enough money to take a plane from Miami to New York, so we all packed into a bus for the two-day trip.

Our story in the United States began in New York in a cold December when we arrived at Port Authority, the bus terminal on 42nd Street, in the middle of the night. I remember looking out the bus window and seeing ominous shadowy figures moving in the darkness, men in large overcoats braced against the cold and wind. You can imagine how different this was from what I was familiar with in green and sunny Pinar del Rio.

We had to get to a place that we knew was called "West Side." Not knowing the transportation system, and too scared to spend our meager funds on a taxi, we walked to the address that had been given to us.

Our relatives had arranged for us to stay in a place they called a "funy roon." This was a small one-room apartment with threadbare furniture, a small refrigerator, and a hot plate with two grills. The room smelled of dust and something else I couldn't recognize. I later realized that smell came from the steam on the radiator, which also made a high-pitched whistling sound whenever we turned it on to heat up the freezing room. The small, bare lightbulb cast an eerie yellow light over the room.

There were mouse traps in several corners of the room, which told us, of course, there were also mice.

There was no bathroom. The toilet was in a tiny enclosure down the hall, and it was shared by the other inhabitants of the floor, which had several "funy roons" on it.

My cousin and I surveyed our new environment and resolved to make the best of it. We were in the United States, which had been our goal. We should consider ourselves lucky, we thought. Things could be a lot worse. Soon, things did get a lot worse.

There was only one bed, and we tucked in for the night. Just a few minutes after turning off the light, we heard the loud clack of the mouse trap snapping closed and a little squeak.

Shortly thereafter, we heard another snap and squeak, then another. Three mice had been caught in traps. I moved to remove the rodents, not sure where I would dump them as I didn't know where the garbage was. *"Déjalo, déjalo,"* Carlos said. *"Lo hacemos mañana."* (Leave it, leave it. We'll worry about it tomorrow.) We went back to sleep.

In the middle of the night, my cousin began to twitch and jerk in bed. *"¿Que te pasa?"* I called out. (What's wrong?)

Carlos said he was being bitten by something. He jumped up and turned on the light. Initially, we didn't see anything, but as we lifted the thin, stained mattress, we saw a swarming pile of bedbugs. *"¡Chinches, coño!"* Carlos yelled when he saw that teeming mass moving in unison.

That was too much. The exhaustion and stress of the previous days crashed down on us. I just stood there transfixed. Carlos sat on the edge of a chair and cried.

That night we slept on the cold hard floor covered with thin blankets. The next day, we found another "funy roon" to stay in. It was equally depressing—but no bedbugs. This room only had a couch, no bed. I had to sleep with my feet to Carlos's head, so we could both fit.

When I learned better English, I wondered why they called those depressing studios "funy roons." What's funny about those rooms, I thought? Later, we learned that what Cubans were calling a "funy roon" to describe a cheap accommodation was actually a mispronunciation of the words "furnished room."

16

In 1962, when I arrived from Cuba in Flushing, Queens, New York, there were already hundreds of Cuban families living in the area. The street I lived on was 41st Avenue, which had buildings on both sides of the street. You could find at least ten Cuban families living in each of these buildings.

As I recall, there were only two major supermarkets servicing the area, and neither one carried the Spanish lines that we used for our cooking. That was key in my first business endeavor.

I was twelve years old, and my uncle knew a Cuban man who was able to supply me with Cuban products that I could sell to the Cuban families in the nearby buildings.

I would go out with a shopping cart and visit the Cuban families in each building. I guess they were happy to be able to buy things that they couldn't find in the supermarkets. Perhaps they may have felt a little sorry for a little boy already trying to earn some money.

Some of the families would purchase *fiao* (on credit), so I had to keep a list of what was owed in a little booklet.

I sold a few products, and here is a list as I remember: Theresa guava paste and *jalea*, Ancel mango paste, *coco rayado*, and *dulce de frutabomba*. *Chorizos Esteves, aceite Carbonel*, and *Galletas La Rosa*. For *Nochebuena* (Christmas Eve), I sold *turrones Sanchis Mira*.

I even sold Cuban LP records, like Beny Moré, Orquesta Aragón, Celia Cruz, and others.

I used the earnings from my sales to buy household things for my parents who arrived in the United States six months after I did.

17

We were a family of eight, and we all came to the United States around the same time.

We ended up in a one-bedroom apartment with a small kitchenette. You can imagine the crowding. Still, we were grateful to be in the U.S.

What I remember the most was seeing the incredible variety and quantity of products in the stores. I felt somehow guilty looking at all that abundance, knowing that people in Cuba didn't even know these products existed, much less have access to them.

18

My family was too poor to have fond memories of Cuba. They were just happy to get out.

My mom worked in a factory in Hartford, Connecticut for four years in freezing weather when she got to the United States. She and my grandparents then came to Union City, New Jersey to reunite with other family members. They moved into a roach-infested, dingy apartment in the run-down part of the city.

Shortly thereafter, my mom got seriously ill. She and my dad, a Spaniard she met in New Jersey, didn't know how they were going to pay the bills, even though they were living with my grandparents.

Eventually, my mom got a job as an embroidery designer in New York City, and my dad, an accountant by trade, managed a local hotel. Little by little, they pulled out of that depressing life and prospered.

19

Life in exile was certainly different in material ways, but I have fond memories of spending a lot more time with my parents and having a much more closely-knit family life.

My parents always displayed a very positive attitude, and I never heard any bitterness, except for everybody always wishing that Castro would drop dead—proof positive that curses and ill thoughts don't work.

20

My father told my mother to leave with me and my sister and that he would join us as soon as he got out. My mother was afraid she might not get another opportunity, so she left with us and her mother—my grandmother— who had already suffered a stroke in Cuba and was partially paralyzed.

That was in 1962. From that time until 1969, my mother did everything she could to get my father out, but nothing ever seemed to work. Finally, late in 1969, my father told my mother that he had met another woman and would not leave Cuba. My mother was devastated and fell into a deep depression. I remember a time when she would spend entire days in bed. About ten years later, my father arrived from Cuba alone. His new wife had left him. He tried to get together with my mother, but she would have none of it.

To make a little more money, my mother worked the night shift at a large credit union because the pay at night was higher. Her job was in downtown Manhattan around the Financial District, and we lived in Brooklyn. She had to travel long distances and would arrive home at weird hours, frozen from the cold. That money, plus some child support and food stamps, helped us survive until my sister and I became adults.

My mother passed away some time ago, but she left us with a solid work ethic and confidence in our ability to endure and overcome any challenge life throws at us.

PART 3 - CULTURAL CONFUSION

PART 3
CULTURAL CONFUSION:
LANGUAGE AND CUSTOMS

1

My mother spoke no English when she arrived, but that never stopped her from navigating her new country. She would just string words together, add a gesture or two, and somehow, she made herself understood.

One day, she needed a lightbulb. The informal word for lightbulb in Spanish is *foco*. She figured many English words just didn't have the vowel sound at the end of the word, like *instituto* in Spanish is "institute" in English, for example, and *restaurante* in Spanish is "restaurant" in English. Therefore, she figured, just remove the "o" from *foco*, and that just might be how you say "lightbulb" in English.

Confident in her ability to overcome this challenge, off she went to the hardware store to get her *foco*. "Pleees, I guana foc," she told the clerk. You can imagine the possible misinterpretation and the look on his face.

"I beg your pardon?" he asked, uncertainly.

"I guana foc," she insisted.

The clerk, by now a bit flustered, mimed for her to point out what she wanted. She pointed to a box of light bulbs.

"Oh!" the clerk exclaimed, "electric lightbulbs."

My mom came back with the box and told us the story. *"¡Imaginate! Jamás en la vida se me hubiera ocurrido 'iletri laibol!'"* (Can you imagine? It never would have occurred to me to say *iletri laibol* (electric lightbulb).

2

My aunt swore by Vick's VapoRub, otherwise referred to as *Bibaporu* by all Cubans, even if they speak perfectly fluent English. If we even looked like we might sneeze, she would lather our chests with the gel and dab a bit into our nostrils to help us breathe.

One day, we got a vaporizer, which came with a special liquid solution to use with it. She didn't know what a vaporizer was for because if we ever needed one, we'd just throw a towel over our heads and inhale hot *Bibaporu*.

My aunt saw the Vicks vaporizer solution and thinking that it was cough syrup, she took a big swig. Lesson learned!

3

My parents arrived from Cuba in October 1963. I guess the tension of leaving was too stressful because five days later my mom went into labor with my older sister, several weeks before she was due. This surprise labor meant my parents were unprepared.

My dad spoke no English but managed to get a taxi. As they got in, he pointed excitedly at my mom's belly and mimed cradling a baby in his arms while my poor mother groaned.

Fortunately, the driver understood, but he drove them to the wrong entrance of Mount Sinai Hospital. A passing nurse recognized the urgency and ran to get a wheelchair.

My sister was almost out by the time they got into the labor room. She was born in less than fifteen minutes.

4

From kindergarten to eighth grade, we had to sing the national anthem every morning. When I went off to high school, I discovered that the first line was not "Oh José, can you see?"

5

My father was applying for a job in the early '60s in Missouri. He was given a cup and asked to provide a sample as part of his hiring process. When he came back with the sample and handed it to the nurse, she was confused. He had spat into the cup, not realizing they wanted a urine sample. The nurse had to explain the particular bodily fluid needed to him.

6

I can't tell you how many stories I've heard throughout my life about the Cuban exiles that mistook the cat food for tuna. I imagine that happened to all immigrants to the United States from non-English-speaking countries.

7

My father-in-law had such a great sense of humor and would keep us laughing with his many stories. I remember he would dramatize his narratives with sound effects and dead-on impersonations. I think he was a frustrated movie director or standup comic.

He would tell us the story of when he worked at a hardware store taking inventory. A lady came up to him and asked for keys. Since he spoke no English, he thought she was saying "kiss," so he was confused by this lady's increasing annoyance and continually repeated request.

8

My mom had studied dentistry in a small town in Georgia and decided to stay in the United States after graduation to establish her practice. She brought her sister and brother-in-law from Cuba in 1963.

My aunt and uncle had to travel around town on local transportation. When they first arrived, they got on a bus and happened to sit in the back row. The driver stopped the bus and told them to move to the front. He told them black people sit in the back of the bus and white people in the front. He asked them to remember this and not be disruptive. That's what the South was like in the early 1960s.

9

My brother-in-law started going to night school as soon as he arrived in the United States from Jovellanos in Matanzas province. He was determined to learn English and to get a good job as soon as he could.

A very gregarious man, he quickly made friends with people in town. He was never concerned about his English and would just jump into the conversation. One day, he and my sister were invited to a Tupperware party (that was popular back then). He got

Tupperware and underwear mixed up and spent the evening talking about his wife's lovely underwear collection. We still laugh about that.

10

On our first Halloween in 1961 in Manhattan, we had no idea of the tradition, but we saw kids dressed in costumes, knocking on doors in our building, and getting candy. We thought it looked like a lot of fun and wanted to do it, too.

We didn't have money for costumes, so we threw sheets over each other and went as a family of ghosts. We knocked on doors and said what we thought the kids were saying, "Chicken Feet!" instead of "Trick or Treat."

When the people opened the doors, they just smiled and gave us candy. Since we didn't know that Halloween was just one day, we thought we could do this at any time. The following weekend, we again dressed up as ghosts and went in search of more candy.

We knocked on the same doors and this time, when the people opened their doors, they explained that Halloween was the previous week. We went home giggling.

A week later, we wanted to go trick or treating yet again, so we dressed up, choose a different set of doors to knock on, and when the confused people opened the door, we told them that our cousin had just come to visit from a place where they didn't have Halloween, and we wanted her to have the experience before she went back. Some people actually gave us candy.

11

Just after I started college, I met a cute guy I really liked. I told my parents I wanted him to be my boyfriend. Always trying to help, my parents suggested I bring him home, so they could subject him to a Cuban charm offensive.

Everyone sat in the living room on our plastic-covered furniture and smiled at each other while my mom served rum and cokes.

After a little small talk to get over the first awkward moments, my father approached the guy and asked him if he liked "pinus." My friend looked confused and a little uncomfortable. Undaunted, my dad leaned closer, nodded enthusiastically and insisted with an encouraging grin, "Jes, jes. I give ju pinus." He shook his fist up and down and opened his hand to reveal the snacks inside. "Oh! Peanuts!" my friend exclaimed.

12

Spanish speakers have trouble mispronouncing the letters "Y" and "J."

I know some people who, even after decades in the United States, when they say "jail," it sounds like "Yale."

I've also heard confusion with the words panty hose and panty house as well as blow dry and blow job.

Of course, there are always giggles when people order "cocks" instead of "Cokes" or order a "shit" cake because they mispronounce "cheese."

Learning a new language when you're already an adult is a challenge. That many exiles pursued language classes at night, frequently after a long day at work, is a testament to their determination to make better lives for themselves and their families.

13

When we arrived from Cuba in August of 1966, my father didn't understand the tipping customs in the United States. We were celebrating a birthday, and it was our first time out in a restaurant.

After dinner, my dad tipped the waiter two nickels. He was happy when we left because he saw the waiter showing the coins to the other waiters and laughing. He thought the waiter was happy; he was probably laughing at how ridiculous the tip was.

14

Some Spanish words have different meanings in different countries in Latin America.

My friend tells the story how, on a business trip to Santa Fe, New Mexico, he decided to stop for lunch at a Mexican restaurant that advertised authentic Mexican cuisine.

When he walked into the restaurant, he noticed the restaurant's "Help Wanted" sign posted in the window by the door. The sign read: *"Necesitamos tortilleras con experiencia"* (Wanted: experienced tortilla makers).

Note: The word *tortillera* means "lesbian" in Cuban slang. You can imagine how surprised Cubans would be when they saw a sign in a restaurant seeking experienced lesbians!

15

Confusion over products was very common among Cubans newly arrived in the United States. Some examples:

I remember the woman who purchased a bottle of lemon juice for cooking, thinking it was lemonade. Of course, she took a swig.

Confectioner's sugar was another mystery, frequently confused with regular sugar.

My mother sent me to the store shortly after coming over in the mid-sixties to get "baki po." I looked in several different locations but returned empty handed. She got upset with me and showed me the little can of baking powder. I had to go back and get it.

Another time, it took me a long time to find the "café mate" my aunt wanted until I figured out she was referring to Coffee Mate creamer.

No Cuban ever referred to Uncle Ben's rice by its brand name of "Uncle Ben's." It was always called Tio Ben (Uncle Ben). When we first arrived, my mother sent me to the store to buy "Tio Ben" rice. My English was still basic. No one understood when I asked for "Tio Ben." I finally located a box and brought it home, and I quickly learned to call it "Uncle Ben's."

My father bought root beer thinking it was real beer. You can imagine his shock at that first taste. I mean, what *is* root beer anyway?

Cracker meal, used for breading, used to come in canisters that resembled Comet or Ajax cleaner. One day, about a month after she arrived from Cuba, I caught my poor sister-in-law cleaning the toilet with cracker meal. She wondered why it wasn't working.

One day, I had to go to our local grocery store to look for toilet paper. We had just arrived from Cuba and my English consisted of literally translating words from the Spanish. I walked in, and I asked for sanitary paper. The clerk showed me tampons, sanitary napkins, and some weird terrycloth thing with straps. I knew he didn't understand, so I looked around until I finally saw a stack of toilet paper rolls in a corner, and I grabbed a roll. Little by little, I learned the names of the products.

And then there was that large collection of white powder in boxes, and you never knew what it was for. Was it baking powder, flour, batter, baker's sugar? How did one distinguish among them without knowing how to read the labels? The pictures helped sometimes, but a picture of a fish on a can was just as likely to be cat food as tuna.

16

One night, my son, a nurse, was speaking with a patient who had just undergone a serious and delicate abdominal procedure. My son told the patient *"Lo vamos a velar está noche,"* (we're going to watch you tonight). Apparently, the patient had a sense of humor and responded, "Do I look that bad?"

Note: The word "watch" can also be translated to "have a wake" depending on the context.

17

My parents came over in 1963. Driving around looking for an apartment, my father would pass by perfectly acceptable buildings. We asked why he wasn't stopping at any of them. In frustration, he pointed to the "vacancy" sign and said, "Can't you see? They're all on vacation!"

18

The word "sheet" is fraught with perilous pronunciations for Spanish speakers.

My mom and I went to Alexander's on Queens Boulevard in Queens, New York to buy bed linens before I got married. She wanted me to have the best.

Throughout the conversation with the salesclerk, my mom referred to the linens as "king sized shits" and "shits with stripes." The salesclerk tried to keep a straight face, and eventually, Mom got just what she wanted. Our sheet buying experience joined our family lore.

My first day teaching I was pointing out instructions to the class and said, "shit of paper" to a group of teenagers. Giggles and guffaws erupted across the class. For the rest of my career, I never repeated that word. Also, I made sure to never say the word "worksheet." Instead, I would always say "handout."

Another "sheet" story is the Cuban who told his American girl friend that he liked to sleep with only a shit on the bed.

19

We flew to Boston right after arriving to Miami. We were hungry because we did not have time to eat between flights and had not had anything to eat for some time.

We had never flown before, so we didn't really know what to expect. When they started serving food on the flight, my father turned it down. He thought we would have to pay for it, and we had no money. We sat there watching the other passenger enjoy their meals while we breathed in the delicious aromas and starved!

20

It took us a while to stop asking for "fried butterflies" at the local Chinese restaurant. That's what we called fried wonton in Cuba, *maripositas.*

21

On one of our first *Nochebuenas* (Christmas Eves) in the United States, my parents invited the American neighbors they'd made friends with to celebrate with us Cuban style. The neighbors brought some of their own traditions too, including Christmas stockings, eggnog, and a mistletoe.

They hung the mistletoe over our dining room doorway but didn't think to explain its significance it to my parents. The kids knew what it was, but my mom had no idea. She assumed it was just a decoration. During the evening, she happened to stand beneath it, and the neighbor came up to her to kiss her.

Surprised, she moved away from the neighbor, who jokingly chased her. Laughing, we explained the tradition to her, and everybody had a good laugh.

22

Our neighbor tells this story about when he came from Cuba to New York City in 1964. He had just gotten a new job way uptown and had to take the subway to work. On the way back, he got off at 110th Street. Going home from there, he got totally lost.

He called his wife who knew the area better. She asked him to look at the street signs and let her know where he was. He said, "I am at the corner of No Exit and One Way."

23

None of us spoke English when we arrived, but I was going to school and learning rapidly.

We had a little cantina service (food delivery). It was my job to wash the containers, a job I hated. My mom would remind me, and I would respond, "I know," with an exasperated sigh. My mom didn't know what that meant. She thought I said, "Ay, no," which means "no way" or "forget it." Of course, she became very upset until I explained I had responded in English, not Spanish.

24

My mother worked in a factory that laid

people off in the summer when she would receive unemployment.

At the unemployment office, they would always require her to answer three questions before they gave her check: what's your name, where do you live, and did you work during the week?

She spoke no English and would memorize the answers to the questions in the order they were asked. One week, they switched the questions and asked first where she lived.

Accustomed to the usual order in which the questions were asked, she answered with her name. It took a while to straighten things out, and she eventually got her check. Thereafter, I or my brother would go with her to translate and avoid confusion.

25

Our neighbor was confused by "Garage Sale" or "Yard Sale." "Why don't they sell the whole house instead?" she asked. She couldn't help but wonder at this strange land.

26

Pastries in a box were a new phenomenon for us when we came from Cuba. We used to see little boxes with pictures of pies or danishes on them, and the product inside was delicious.

A few weeks after we arrived, my aunt and I went to the supermarket where we bought a box that we thought had a cherry pie inside. The box had a picture of a fat, delicious-looking cherry pie in a plastic bag on it.

As soon as we got home, my aunt took two plates and a knife to cut the cherry pie in half so we could share. We were so disappointed to discover that the box only had plastic bags inside and no pie!

27

The teachers in my public school in Miami were surprised see how Cuban parents gave them the authority to discipline the kids. Cuban parents were accustomed to sending their kids to Catholic schools where corporal punishment was accepted.

Even though it was explained to parents that physically disciplining children was not acceptable in the United States, they still wanted to give teachers permission to do so if they thought it was necessary.

I once saw a father complain to the principal, saying the teachers were not doing their job of properly disciplining his child.

28

One day, my mom and my sister were leaving for the park, and my mom asked my sister where her father was. At this point, we were switching back and forth from English to Spanish without even thinking about it.

My sister responded, *"Él dice que maybe viene."* (He says maybe he'll come.)

My mom got furious and said, "Why does he always have to be inviting strange people? And who is this guy 'Maybe' that I don't know?"

29

I must have eaten something that didn't agree with me because I had a bad case of allergies and hives and didn't go to school. The next day, my mother wrote a note to the teacher saying I had been "intoxicated." Of course, they immediately called my home and asked my mother to come in for a meeting.

Note: The word *intoxicada* means having an allergic reaction in Spanish.

30

I once told a classmate to stop molesting me, which got the attention of the whole classroom. I only meant for him to stop bothering me.

Note: The expression "to bother" is *molestar* in Spanish.

31

My grandmother, a religious woman, thought that Thanksgiving Day and the Thanksgiving Day Parade were in commemoration of a saint, "San Given." She believed this for years, and we were not aware of it. One day, she went to a botánica (a store selling religious articles) to look for a candle to commemorate San Given. *He must be very powerful since so many people make such a big fuss over him,* she thought.

32

We were living in Weehawken, New Jersey. My brother-in-law had just become an American citizen.

One day, we were driving down Bergenline Avenue. We had to make a turn, and there was a line of cars also waiting to merge. Just as we were getting ready to turn, a delivery van with the words *Los Hermanos Cubanos* (The Cuban Brothers) written on the front cut in front of us. My brother-in-law, who had only been a citizen for a few days, grimaced and said, "These Cubans don't know how to drive!"

33

My recently arrived parents had to travel to Miami from Tampa. They passed a catfish restaurant and laughing, they joked about what kind of restaurant it could be: a restaurant for cats where they served fish? Words like "catfish" when translated literally can sound bizarre and funny to the foreign ear.

34

The objective of *cubiletes,* (a dice game), is to get four aces. My dad spent time explaining the game to our bewildered Bahamian friends telling them they had to get four asses.

35

We would drive down from Boston to Miami every year. As we arrived at the Miami Beach area after the long journey, my mom would open her arms expansively and declare that we had arrived in Miami Bitch!

36

I looked for a job in the classifieds when I first started to work in the United States in the early 1960s. I found one that seemed a good fit. My English was still not particularly good, and when I read the last line, "Good at figures," I assumed they wanted someone with a good figure. This was not an unreasonable assumption, given that this was sixty years ago. Also, I was new to the country and the culture, so I didn't really question it.

Shortly thereafter, I was chatting with my cousin who had been in the United States longer than I had, and I mentioned the job. I told her I declined to apply because I was a little heavy.

My cousin explained the ad meant good with numbers. I did apply for the job and got it. I worked there for five years before moving on to a better job.

37

When I was a little girl, I went to Saint Augustine, Florida with my parents to spend a couple of days on a little getaway.

We drove by a house that was being tented for termites and thought it was a circus. We made plans to return on the way back and go to the circus. When we returned, of course we couldn't find it because the tent had been removed.

It wasn't until much later when we saw other houses being tented in Miami that we figured out it wasn't a circus.

38

A friend of mine who spoke very little English got a job at a factory in Flushing, New York.

Before starting his shift, his supervisor gave him a lengthy explanation of what his duties entailed. The supervisor then asked, "You follow me?" My friend said yes and proceeded to follow the supervisor all over the factory, logically assuming there would be further training.

After several minutes with my friend following him around, the supervisor asked my friend if he wanted something. "Ju say follow me. I follow ju," he responded. The supervisor laughed and explained that "you follow me" was a way of asking if he understood what he said, not a command to go everywhere he went right behind him!

39

My aunt was a twenty-three-year-old farm girl from Gibara flying to Miami alone in 1960. On the plane, they gave her coffee with two little cups of creamers. She tasted the coffee and hated it. She still says it was the worst coffee she ever tasted. She opened the creamer cups and drank the creamers down, thinking either these Americans don't drink much milk, or this airline is really cheap.

40

I remember when people asked me if I wanted my meat "well done." I assumed they were asking if I wanted it cooked properly. I couldn't understand why they were asking me that. Of course, I wanted it well done! Why would I want it done badly?

I also remember when the salesclerks at my new job in Daytona Beach invited me to lunch. When it came time for dessert, I told the waitress I wanted apple pie. She asked if I wanted it a la mode. Feeling lost, I asked the girls what she meant by that, and they said, "Ice cream on top." I told the waitress, "I want apple pie without the mode."

41

When my cousin came from Cuba, she got a job as a cashier in a discount store. Her son thought he was being funny and taught her how to count in English and to say, "fuky" instead of "forty." One day, her supervisor caught her giving change saying "...fuky-seven, fuky-eight..." Her supervisor corrected her, and we still laugh about that today.

42

When we left Cuba, we lived in Maryland for a bit. One day, my mom bought some cute cookies home. We realized they were cat treats and explained it to her. She told us the box of "cookies" was so pretty and dainty with a picture of a kitten on it, so she had to buy it.

Imagine coming from a country where food was scarce and then realizing that pet food is sold in pretty boxes in the United States.

Even today, I'll walk into one of these huge American supermarkets and think to myself, *"¡Si la gente en Cuba viera esto!"* (If the people in Cuba could see this!)

43

When we first came to the United States, my brother and I went to a Japanese restaurant. They served us a fragrant bowl of water which was for us to dip our fingers in and dry them off with a hot towel before the meal. My brother was about to take a spoonful, thinking it was soup, before a waiter stopped him. "It smelled so good I almost ate it," he said.

That was the same night he ate a big spoonful of wasabi, thinking it was guacamole. He has stayed away from Japanese restaurants ever since.

44

When my father-in-law first came from Cuba, he went looking to buy beer but wasn't sure where he could buy it. He saw a sign he recognized: "Supermarket." He went in and looked all around the place for the beer section until he realized it was a Pet Supermarket.

45

It was Christmas time, and my uncle went out and got some Christmas cards for his friends and family. The poor guy wasn't sure what he was buying. He ended up sending all sorts of cards, none of which were Christmas cards. He sent out Chanukah cards, sympathy cards, and anniversary cards.

For several years after that, my family decided to make this a family tradition. They would also send each other non-Christmas cards during Christmas, in solidarity with my uncle. Our kids also do this, and it is now a really odd and funny family tradition.

46

In my grade school class at Our Lady of Fatima in Manhattan, the nuns referred to the bathroom as "the lavatory." I barely understood or spoke English. When they asked who wanted to use the lavatory, I thought they were saying laboratory, but I didn't know what that even was.

I wanted to use the bathroom, so didn't raise my hand. Later, when I asked to use the bathroom, the teacher was upset and asked why I didn't go when she'd asked earlier.

I also heard kids saying that they had to go to the restroom. I remember thinking it was so thoughtful and civilized of the school to have a place where students could rest if they were tired during the day!

Even little things like this caused confusion.

47

We managed to bring our purebred female poodle, Lola, with us from Cuba. She went through Venezuela and arrived in Miami looking sad and tired, poor thing.

My grandfather, who spoke no English except for the bad words, walked her every day.

A neighbor who had dogs and showed them at the local dog shows referred to Lola as a bitch. My grandfather couldn't figure out what he meant because the only meaning he knew for that word would have been mean and rude, yet the man was being friendly and smiling.

When he came home, he told me what the man had called Lola. I explained that "bitch" meant "female dog" and was perfectly acceptable.

48

One day, I got a bad chest cold, and my mother stayed home with me. The next day when she got to work, her boss asked her why she had been absent. She answered in her very broken English, "my doter haf muy bad constipation." The boss was taken aback, but in Spanish, *constipado* means congested as with a cold.

49

We were shopping at Montgomery Ward. My father needed a pair of pants or slacks. The salesclerk understood "pans" and sent him over to the cookware department where he could find his pans.

50

My aunt took her young daughter everywhere as an interpreter. One day, they went to the doctor who asked the daughter, "How are her bowels?" Confused and with a strange look on her face, my cousin asked her mom, "Mom, the doctor wants to know if you know your vowels." Equally perplexed, my aunt responded, "A, E, I, O, U."

51

It took me forever to understand the expression "up a creek without a paddle." I was picturing us in a canoe and could not for the life of me figure out what people were trying to say.

Other weird American expressions that always stumped me when I tried to translate them in my mind were:

"All the tea in China."

"Break a leg."

"He is not a big fan."

Someone is "a wet blanket."

"Spill the beans."

"A bird in the hand is worth two in the bush."

Granted, Cuban expressions are legendary for their own inscrutable meanings or so non-Cubans tell me. But for me, American expressions "take the cake."

52

I don't know if this silly story is true, but I've heard it so many times from so many different people, maybe there is something to it.

A man tried to buy a Coca-Cola from a vending machine. He was short ten cents and the machine flashed the word, "Dime." My friend whispered to the machine, "Una Coca-Cola, por favor."

Note: The word *dime* means "tell me" in Spanish.

53

I used to work at a credit union, and when clients were late on their payments, they got a delinquent notice.

One day, a Cuban client came in really upset. He was a big man with a cowboy hat and cowboy boots. He demanded to know why the company was calling him a "delinquent" and insisted on talking to the manager. He thought his character was being insulted.

54

My cousin came from Cuba at age fifteen, by which time it was already more difficult to learn a new language. She had to be tutored separately in order to take part in her age-appropriate class. Her teacher took it upon herself to tutor her during lunch in the teacher's lounge.

One day, the teacher was called away to the office. She told my cousin to watch her purse. My cousin thought the teacher had said, "Wash my purse." My cousin thought the request a bit odd, but she figured it was some American thing. Wisely, she waited until the teacher returned before taking everything out of the purse and washing it.

55

I always got a kick out of the translated expression "between and drink a chair" *(entre y tome asiento).*

Note: The phrase "Enter and take a seat" translates literally in Spanish into *"Between and drink a chair."*

56

I often imagined that some of the Americans felt a little overwhelmed by the wave of Cubans that had suddenly arrived in their midst. Many Americans made an effort to communicate with the new arrivals. Others, not so much.

Two simple stories come to mind. The first is about the repairman that had to get inside my house. He asked if we had a dog. I thought he meant door, and I said yes. He asked if it was a big dog. I said yes. I invited him in, pointed to the garage door, and said, "Look, big." He shook his head, then "woofed," and I finally understood he was talking about a dog.

The other story is when I asked for a wine-colored bag I had seen in the store's brochure. The clerk said there was no such color. I had to go and get another copy of the brochure and point it out to him. "This color is burgundy," he said. He just didn't make an effort to understand. Sometimes that made life just a little bit more difficult for us, unnecessarily.

57

I remember there was a sweet older gay couple that had just arrived from Cuba living next door, Felipe and Efrain. To make ends meet, they would babysit my sister and me while our parents went to work. Felipe was an excellent cook, and he would make lunch for us.

Felipe frequently made *picadillo* (a ground beef dish). Even today, I can remember the taste of his picadillo. It didn't taste anything like what my mom made, but we ate it. He would mix it with tomato sauce, add onions and spices, but it still didn't taste like my mom's picadillo.

After weeks of eating picadillo, one day I saw Felipe take the ground beef out of a box that was in his kitchen cabinet. Even as a young child, I knew that ground beef should come from a refrigerator.

I took a closer look at the box and saw it was dog food! Back then, a certain brand of dog food came in boxes, and the food was formed to look like ground beef patties.

Poor Felipe. He was appalled that he had been feeding us and Efrain dog food and was afraid he would lose his babysitting job.

My mom asked him if he didn't think it odd that the meat was not refrigerated. He answered that he thought it was some clever American invention.

58

My mom was a beautician. She was also religious and belonged to an evangelical church in the neighborhood. She was strict about us using bad words, so my sister and I were not allowed to call each other a "pain in the ass" because our mom would reprimand us. Instead, we switched to using the term "pain in the neck." I guess we must have confused her.

One day at her job, she was finishing a short haircut. She needed to ask her customer if she wanted her to shave her neck. Instead, she asked the woman if she wanted her ass shaved. Fortunately, the lady was very good customer, and they laughed it off.

That happened so many years ago, and I still get a kick out of it.

Coincidentally, I married the son of my mother's customer. We had two children and have been very happy. We still tell that story, and our kids get a big laugh out of it.

59

I had gone to an American school in Cuba and spoke a little English, so I was the translator.

My mother took me to a basement department store in Boston to buy me a coat for our first winter. I found one I liked, and it was priced at fifteen dollars. My mom told me to offer the sales lady ten dollars. I knew this wasn't going to work, but she insisted.

Reluctantly, I relayed the message to the sales lady. I had to repeat it several times because she had no idea what I was trying to say. Of course, she refused.

I had to explain to my mother that in the United States it was not normal to haggle in a department store. She responded, "Try and you might fail. But don't try and you're guaranteed to fail." Her advice has served me well over the years, just not for bargaining in U.S. department stores.

60

Back in the seventies, there was a county court in Coral Gables where judges heard traffic cases.

The court always had interpreters because of the many non-English-speaking Cubans who continued to arrive.

One of these interpreters, Armando, was also a court clerk. He had already been in the United States for some time and had a very peculiar sense of style. He would wear polka dot blazers with striped shirts, brightly colored pants with little designs on them, colorful socks, and a wide variety of bow ties. We often wondered if he was just colorblind or honestly thought he was stylish. People would stop by the court just to see what he was wearing that day.

His clerking style was no less unusual. He would confuse the files and always hand the judge, a Chinese woman, documents that would mess up the cases.

One day, a lady came to state her case, explaining that a motorcycle cop chased her suddenly, but she used the slang *caballito* (little horse) to mean motorcycle cop. Armando translated for the judge saying that the woman claimed to have been chased by a little horsey. The judge and the Cuban crowd exploded in laughter as the combination of Armando's hilarious translation and bizarre clothing was too much!

61

I was five or six when we came to Atlanta, Georgia from Oriente Province. Of course, none of us spoke or read English. My grandfather would babysit me while my parents worked. One night, I got my hands on a box of "chocolates" from the medicine cabinet. My grandfather and I enjoyed several pieces of these chocolates before my parents came home.

A few hours later, my poor grandfather couldn't stop going to the bathroom, and my mom was concerned he might be sick. She asked my grandfather, *"¿Que comiste que te cayó mal?"* (What did you eat that didn't agree with you?) My grandfather told her I had given him "chocolates."

My increasingly confused mother asked me where I had gotten the chocolates. I gave her the box of Ex-lax.

62

Everyone has a favorite story about the silly mistakes people made when going for the American citizen exam. Here's mine.

I knew a guy that went for the exam. He had studied a lot but was nervous. When they asked him the name of the first president of the United States, he said George Washington Bridge. He managed to compose himself; everyone was amused and understood his jitters, and he passed the test.

63

Shortly after we arrived from Jovellanos, I got a job in a factory. We were expected to clean our workstations. I guess my supervisor didn't think I was cleaning hard enough and asked that I use some elbow grease.

Not wanting to get reprimanded, I went in search of elbow grease. I located the floor manager who was a nice old guy from Nicaragua and told him what I was looking for. He was not aware of that product, so together we went to the main supply depot to ask where we could get some.

By now, I was starting to get nervous that I would get in trouble with my supervisor for not following instructions.

In the supply depot, the staff had a good laugh and explained to both me and the floor manager what it meant. Who knew?

64

We settled in Brooklyn, New York. We were anxious to fit in and did everything we could to learn English quickly. We practiced reading and speaking English only.

On the weekends, we would go into Manhattan by subway. We really liked going to Delancey Street because that's where the bargains were.

At the subway, we climbed the stairs to the elevated tracks. At every other step, we saw warnings we couldn't understand. We were stumped! The warning: NO FUME! It took us a while to realize it was Spanish, and no translation was needed: "No Smoking!"

65

When we first came from Cuba, we ended up in, of all places, Schenectady, New York in the middle of winter. After being there for about three months, we were really missing Cuba, and we were sick of American food. When the weather got warmer, we decided to wander around the area and get to know it better. We took a bus to the next town where we heard there was discount shopping.

Walking around, we got hungry. My mom and sister were window shopping, so I walked ahead to find a local restaurant for us to have lunch. Twenty minutes later, I found myself in front of this little hole-in-the-wall joint. I was surprised to see it had photos of food that I recognized. I was even more surprised when I saw the restaurant's name, La Bodeguita del Medio!

We spent hours eating and drinking the most delicious *moros, ropa vieja, croqueticas, frituritas de bacalao, platano maduro, tostones, natilla, flan,* and copious amounts of mojitos. We were so happy to have located a Cuban restaurant. We continued to patronize the restaurant until my dad got a job in Union City, and we moved.

66

I was in the third grade, and we were having a class party. The teacher asked me to bring candy. I told my mom, and she went to the grocery store and brought Smith Brothers brand cough drops, the one with pictures of two bearded old guys on the package.

Fortunately, I looked at the package and realized what they were. I would have been a laughingstock if I showed up in school with cough drops.

My mom saved the day. That night, we made merengue, and I brought the delicious sugary treat to school, telling the kids this was a special Cuban candy. I was the hit of the party. My mom was really special.

67

I went to a birthday party at my friend's apartment in New York with my grandmother as a chaperone.

We were still learning English. My friend was telling me a story of a situation that she was embarrassed about. We were around fourteen years old. My grandmother was listening, and she asked my friend what she was talking about. My grandmother didn't speak a word of English, and my friend translated the word "embarrassed" as *embarazada* (pregnant). My grandmother looked like she might faint, and I had to do some quick translating and explaining to reassure her.

68

My mom used to work in a factory in Brooklyn when we came from Cuba. One day, two ladies at work had a big argument, and my mom was telling me the story. She said the women were screaming at each other and that she didn't know who they were, but she thought one of them was called "Sara Bambi." Of course, she had heard one call the other "son of a bitch."

69

I remember going to a kid's party and not knowing how to play spin the bottle. I really wanted to learn because I saw other guys kissing the girls, and I wanted to do that too, but I was also afraid of making a fool of myself. I learned quickly. I've since made up for it and kissed many a girl.

70

Years ago, when you wanted to call someone long distance, you had to place a call and wait for the operator to call you back and connect the call. I would place a call to my sister with an operator to "Flora Verdail." Eventually, I figured out how to pronounce "Fort Lauderdale."

71

I remember going to our first American birthday party. Anxious to make sure I would fit in, my mom had bought me a pretty party dress of blue tulle with pink satin ribbons. I had the little ankle socks with colored trim and *zapaticos de charol* (patent leather shoes). When I got to the party, all the other kids were running around in jeans and tennis shoes.

It took a while for us to adapt to the American informal style of dress.

72

A friend of mine arrived in the United States from Santa Clara, Cuba where she had been a receptionist in a doctor's office. She managed to get a job fairly quickly and was very happy with her new position assisting in an ophthalmologist office. She was going to school at night to improve her English.

The people at her office encouraged her to practice speaking English with them every chance they got.

One Friday, at the end of the day, she was explaining something to her boss who told her, "Oh, get outta here!" My friend was shocked.

She didn't know what to make of this. She called me and repeated the story to get my opinion. I laughed and explained this was just another one of those inscrutable American expressions that did not mean what they said, and the boss was just playing along and pretending not to believe what she was saying.

73

My mom went to work at the factory with a toothache because she had no choice. Her boss, an older Jewish guy who spoke a little bit of about half a dozen languages, asked her in broken Spanish, *"¿Por que cara larga?"* (Why the long face?)

My mom responded that she had a pain in her teets!

Her boss burst out laughing, and she was furious.

74

My dad had spent about forty-five years in the United States when he discovered that "No Loitering" did not mean that there were no Lottery tickets sold at that location. It had never occurred to him to even question that.

75

My parents had to drive to Canada from Providence, Rhode Island in order to get their permanent residency in 1962. They were checking out of the hotel and decided to have breakfast first.

While my dad went to check out, my mother, a religious evangelist who was against any use of alcohol, went to the restaurant.

When my dad returned, he found my mother sitting at the table with a large glass of cold beer in front of her.

"What's that?" he asked.

"I don't know," she replied. "I told the waiter I wanted juice pear!" She had translated literally from the Spanish and mispronounced. We guess the waiter heard "just beer." She had been too shy about her

English to point out the mistake to the waiter, so she just stayed there with her beer.

76

I remember a family that arrived from Guanabacoa with two little kids, ages four and five. None of them spoke English. The little ones started in day care and within just a few months were speaking English with the other kids and with each another.

As most non-English-speaking parents did with their English-speaking kids, their mother started taking them to the store with her to serve as interpreter. One day, the oldest boy told me with an exasperated look on his face. "I'm tired of going with my mom to all these places and being her talker!"

77

My English was basic at best. I remember trying to explain to someone that my uncle had been a fireman when he was younger before coming from Cuba. Instead, what I said was that my uncle had been a "bomber." It took a while and a lot of pantomime for me to explain what I meant.

Note: Fireman is *bombero* in Spanish.

78

My dad ate pastrami sandwiches every day for lunch for the longest time.

He didn't know the food truck at the factory he worked for had other choices, and actually, that was all he could say in English. Once he learned more English, he never had another pastrami sandwich again.

I later learned this was the case with many Cubans. Outside the home, once they learned the word for something, they ate the same thing over and over again, either because it was cheap and they were afraid to overspend, or they didn't know how to ask for something else.

79

I was born in the United States, but I had a lot of cousins who came over in the '60s and early 70s. I remember a lot of them would get a box of food once a month from the *refugio,* the government entity that provided food staples for refugees. There would be staples like flour, sugar, raisins, and big blocks of American cheese. They would also get a big can of peanut butter. They had no idea what it was, but they really grew to love it and called it "peena boota."

They were grateful they were getting this food for free, which allowed them to save money and get ahead.

80

When I was a little boy, we lived in the Bronx. When I first went to school in 1963, I remember one day our teacher asked us what we'd had for breakfast. When it came to my turn, I told her, "Toast with butter and coffee with milk." She was surprised that my parents would give a child coffee.

The school thought it appropriate to call my parents in for a meeting. My father, who never learned English, came to the school and explained to the school's vice-principal that we were Cuban, and for us, this was a standard breakfast. I love telling this story and always get a chuckle out of it.

81

I grew up in Queens, New York. My mom would give me a thermos with rice and beans or *croqueticas de pollo* (chicken croquettes). Those were delicious options compared to the American food in the cafeteria. The other kids would smell the aroma and wonder what I was eating.

As time passed, I began to share my meals with the other kids who loved it. Eventually, the kids wanted my food, too! Those meals were instrumental in my blending in at my new school.

82

When my dad, a resourceful man with a sense of humor, first came to the United States, he went one day to the grocery store butcher to buy a chicken to make soup.

He didn't know the English word for "chicken," so, always happy to communicate however possible, he flapped his arms and clucked to get the butcher to understand what he wanted.

The butcher, laughing at this show, just happened to also be Cuban. He clapped his hands and said, *"¡Bravo! ¡Excelente interpretación de un pollo!"* (Bravo! Excellent impersonation of a chicken!)

My dad and the butcher became great friends.

EPILOGUE

These personal stories give us a glimpse of the power of the human spirit to transcend an upheaval like the Cuban Revolution and exile to a new and foreign country. The stories celebrate the people who lived them: their strength, their courage, their sense of humanity, and even their sense of humor in the face of enormous obstacles.

May we never forget these people and the critical help of the countries that opened their doors to them.

ABOUT THE AUTHOR

Cuban-American Talek Nantes is an author, digital content creator, and founder of the travel blog, www.travelswithtalek.com. Half of her family came from Cuba in the early 1950s and the other half came a decade later. She has always harbored a passion for her heritage and all things Cuban.

Talek's work has appeared in numerous publications including Atlas Obscura, Audley Travel, Matador Network, Go World Travel, Nomadic Matt, and Reader's Digest.

An avid traveler, Talek's personal and professional background have led her to visit over 110 countries. She has lived and worked throughout the world and speaks several languages. Talek has an MBA as well as a master's degree in International Relations from the University of Pennsylvania.

She lives with her husband in New York City and Miami.

Follow Talek Nantes at:
www.travelswithtalek.com
www.facebook.com/travelswithtalek
Travelswithtalek@travelstalek
www.pinterest.com/travelstalek
www.instagram.com/travelswithtalek

ACKNOWLEDGMENTS

With deep appreciation for all the people who shared their experiences so we would never forget.